# What to Charge

## Pricing Strategies for Freelancers and Consultants

# What to Charge

## Pricing Strategies for Freelancers and Consultants

Laurie Lewis

ALETHEIA
Publications

Lewis, Laurie
What to charge : pricing strategies for freelancers and consultants

Library of Congress Catalog Card Number: 99-75382
ISBN: 1-929129-00-9

Cover design: Bart Solenthaler
Interior design and composition: Guy J. Smith
Copyeditor: David R. Hall
Indexer: Judy Lyon Davis

Aletheia Publications, Inc.
46 Bell Hollow Rd.
Putnam Valley, NY 10579

Printed in Canada

10 9 8 7 6 5 4 3 2 1

*In memory of my parents,*
*with gratitude for the special ways they shaped my life—*

*My father,*
*who taught me that words can be as sweet as dessert.*
*My mother,*
*who knew the value of dreams.*

# Acknowledgments

When my good friend and fellow freelancer David R. Hall first suggested that I write a book about pricing, I didn't take him seriously. But he wouldn't let me brush aside the notion so easily. Dave provided suggestions and examples and, more important, encouragement throughout the process and made a lasting imprint on the finished product by copyediting the manuscript.

To prepare the index, I called on Judy Lyon Davis. I have long admired Judy's businesslike approach to her freelance indexing services and often consult her when I have concerns about the most professional way to handle troublesome situations. I am honored that she agreed to index this book.

I am indebted to Melanie Fuller, who graciously undertook the task of poring over the *Encyclopedia of Associations* and spent hours on the phone confirming the information for the resource appendix.

I thank my agent, Dominick Abel, who believed that the world was ready for a book on pricing strategies for the self-employed. And I am grateful to Carolyn and Guy Smith of

Aletheia Publications, who turned my manuscript into the handsome book you hold in your hands today.

Popular lore maintains that the freelancer's life is a solitary one. Not so in my experience. Throughout my career as an independent business owner, other freelancers have generously shared tips and tales with me. I have learned from their triumphs and disappointments and have incorporated many of their experiences into this book. I bow in gratitude to all my self-employed colleagues, far too numerous to mention by name, who have shared ideas that make my business successful and who gave me examples worthy of inclusion in this volume.

What would a freelance business be without someone on the other side of the assignment desk? For the most part, I have been fortunate to have wonderful clients, whom I thank not only for the work they have given me over the years but for the positive experiences that came back to life with this book. I also acknowledge the clients that proved to be unsatisfying work partners, because through them I learned the other lessons shared in these pages.

# CONTENTS

# 1

## The Big Dilemma

When Quentin got caught in a company's downsizing, he decided to strike out on his own and become a consulting engineer. Two years later, he grossed $17,000 more than he had earned in his last year on staff. What's more, he did it without working weekends, which had become a habit at the company. In fact, Quentin found that he can make more money working 30 hours a week as his own boss than he could working 50 hours a week for somebody else.

But it took him a while to reach this point. Initially, whenever a potential client inquired about his fee, he'd hem and haw and finally sputter out a figure. He found himself always worrying that the rate he quoted would be so high that he'd lose the job or so low that he'd live to regret it. Indeed, once he did commit himself to a project at a ridiculously low rate for the effort involved, then kicked himself as he ate his losses.

Before long, however, Quentin arrived at some steps that changed his business from one that was just muddling along into an enterprise that became the envy of all his self-employed friends. Among his actions were these smart moves:

1

- He made an effort to *find out the going rate* for different types of work. He spoke with colleagues in the field (a.k.a. the competition) and honed his skills at interviewing potential clients so that he could identify their budgetary restraints before becoming too involved.

- Quentin experimented with *different methods of pricing*. Instead of always quoting an hourly fee or accepting a client's offer, he sometimes charged a per diem rate. Sometimes he arranged a retainer with a steady client. He learned to calculate project rates so that jobs would be profitable.

- He changed his *method of record keeping*. Instead of just noting the hours he worked each day, Quentin began to log his time by the tasks that he performed. This method of record keeping had several advantages, the most important being that he was able to calculate more realistic project rates.

- Quentin became a *tough negotiator*. He learned never to quote a price until he carefully thought through a job. Before talking money with the client, he figured out exactly what he wanted and needed to make, how low he was willing to go, and what he expected from the client if he couldn't get top dollar.

- At the end of every job, he *analyzed his pricing decisions*. He calculated how much he could have earned if he had charged on a different basis. At the end of the year, he tallied his earnings from each client and analyzed all his clients side by side. This process enabled him to weed out low-profit situations and raise his rates.

The time-tested strategies that made Quentin's business a financial success are described in detail in this book. The book's goal is to give you, the self-employed professional, techniques to take the guesswork out of pricing.

## About the Rates in This Book

If you're looking simply for a list of rates to charge for particular services, you'll not find them here. Although fee schedules may sometimes be useful starting points, they are not very practical in the long run. Fees can vary tremendously—even for the same work—depending on the type of client you are serving, where you do business, and the special talents you bring to the job.

Instead, this book offers something far more valuable than rate lists: strategies to make your rates fair for the jobs you undertake and to help your business thrive. The methods described in this book are tried and true. They've made me a successful freelance editor and writer, made Quentin richer than any staff job could, and will help you maximize your earnings, too.

Even though it focuses on strategies, a book about pricing must of necessity cite some fees. The rates in the examples here are by no means meant to be the amounts you should charge, and are for illustrative purposes only. The fees given are not the highest ones for a particular type of work, or even the average. They are simply fees that one businessperson charges one client.

An example might state that somebody charges $50 an hour for a particular service. If you are a freelance proofreader working in the publishing industry, this rate will seem extraordinarily high. If you offer consulting services to top executives at *Fortune* 500 companies, the identical charge will seem pathetically low. Every field has a range of typical rates, which vary greatly even within a particular specialty. You'll learn here how to determine the appropriate range for the services you provide.

## Who Will Find This Book Useful?

The assumption throughout is that most readers are professional freelancers and consultants who offer services rather than products. The typical reader probably is a sole proprietor who runs a company of one from a home-based office. However, if you have employees or if you make or sell products, you also will find these strategies useful. Just be sure to allow for your overhead of wages, inventory, and rent and shipping costs, as appropriate, when determining your final charges.

As Juliet told Romeo, "That which we call a rose by any other name would smell as sweet." I have used several names to refer to the sweet ranks of entrepreneurs: *freelancer, consultant, independent contractor,* and *self-employed professional.* No matter what label you prefer, this book is for you if you run your own service-oriented business.

Regardless of the nature of the business, all consultants face the same dilemma: what to charge. Even freelancers who have been in the game for years still worry from time to time about their rates. The question *how much should I charge?* may take various forms, depending on the specific situation:

- Am I asking enough for this job?

- Will I lose the job if I ask for more?

- Should I charge by the hour? Assess a flat project fee? Use some other method?

- Can I charge a particular client top dollar, since I know that the corporate pockets are deep?

- If I charge a small nonprofit operation less than my usual rate, will I set a bad precedent?

- How often can I raise my rates? By how much?

Answers to these and many other questions that bother newcomers and old pros alike will be found in the following pages.

## Who Am I to Tell You What to Charge?

Like you, I am a self-employed freelance professional, an independent contractor who runs a consulting business. I still worry from time to time that I might be asking too much for a job or, more likely, charging too little. But what to charge has become less of a dilemma since I have learned to consistently apply the techniques described in this book.

I have shared these strategies in workshops with fellow freelance writers, editors, proofreaders, and the like. Their feedback has been overwhelmingly positive:

- "You've taken the mystery out of pricing!"

- "Since I started keeping work logs the way you suggest, I don't panic when I have to give an estimate for a complicated job."

- "By saying 'no' the right way to a client who is not offering enough, I sometimes get the job at a rate that works out well for me. I'm happy, and so is the client."

- "Before taking your course, I didn't analyze my earnings after completing a job. It doesn't take long, and it sure provides insights. I feel confident raising my rates based on these analyses."

My own experience, the comments of freelancers who have taken my workshops, and conversations with other consultants in a variety of fields have convinced me that these strategies work. I am certain that if you apply these principles to your own pricing decisions, what to charge will no longer seem like a major dilemma.

# 2

# Not Just by the Hour

A T ITS simplest, the question *how much should you charge?* consists of two more specific questions:

- What method of pricing should you use?
- What dollar rate should you assess?

The broader question actually comprises many other points, which will be explored in later chapters. But these are the two concerns of most consultants when a client asks, "How much will you charge?"

Before focusing on pricing options for individual assignments, look for a moment at the broader picture. How much do you want to earn each month? What would you like your annual income to be? Unless you structure your business to pay yourself a salary (which most sole proprietorships do not do), your income will be less steady than that of an employee on staff. Still, you'll want to have monthly and annual income goals: how much you need to meet your living expenses, pay your taxes, enjoy a vacation, save for retirement, salt away cash for major expenditures

7

like a new home or college for your children, and build a safety cushion to tide you over in a bad year. You need to consider these goals when you set your rates.

## Forget the Past

Some people starting their own business decide to base their freelance rates on their earnings at their last staff job. This is a bad move. Translating previous annual income as a staffer into an equivalent hourly rate fails to consider what life as an independent contractor entails. Consider these realities of self-employment:

- You cannot assume that you will be working forty hours a week every week. Some weeks will be much slower than others.

- Many of the hours you work will not be billable. Whom are you going to invoice for the hours you spend prospecting for new clients? For the time you need to investigate, purchase, and learn to use new equipment or software?

- When you were on staff, your salary probably covered at least three or four weeks when you were not working: your vacation, paid holidays, and days when you called in sick. As a self-employed person, you earn money only when you work. If you want to, you can take off a week to go skiing in January and another week in June to sit on the beach; you can enjoy a four-day Thanksgiving weekend; and you can stay in bed with the flu. But don't expect a paycheck when you return to work.

- In addition to paying for several weeks off, employers offer other perks, such as insurance. Independent contractors, on the other hand, have to pay for their own insurance: medical, dental, disability, life. Even if you opt for a bare-bones approach with only major medical coverage and can join a managed care plan with group rates, you'll have to fork over a minimum of $2,500 a year. Your costs will be substantially higher if you are buying health insurance for your entire family or are purchasing dental, disability, and life insurance. Depending on the type of services you offer, you may need liability insurance as well. And you may have to take out other insurance that was unnecessary when you worked for someone else—for example, a special rider to cover property used in your business, such as a personal computer.

- Employers are required to deduct payroll taxes and pay half the Social Security premium. When you become your own employer, your Social Security premium automatically doubles: It now includes both the portion you used to pay as an employee and your own contribution as the employer of yourself. You'll also have to keep enough cash on hand to pay quarterly estimates of your annual income taxes. When you were on staff, these taxes were deducted from your paycheck.

- Your income will have to cover not only your living expenses but also your business expenses. At a minimum, you should expect $5,000 to $10,000 in start-up costs. The low-end figure will barely pay for business cards and stationery, a business telephone and message-taking mechanism or service, and a computer with software. If you decide to rent office space, hire help, or maintain inventory, you'll have substantial ongoing expenses once your business gets rolling.

All this means that if you want an annual income equivalent to what you earned as an employee, you should plan to charge much more per hour than you earned on staff. You might want to double your hourly income at your last staff job so that you have enough to cover dry spells, nonbillable hours, and time off, and to pay your insurance, taxes, and other business expenses. How to determine whether this initial figure is a realistic hourly rate will be explored in Chapter 4, which explains how to identify the going rate for your type of work.

On the other hand, you don't have to stick with an hourly fee. Many other pricing options are available for the independent contractor. The rest of this chapter examines the pros and cons of various methods of pricing.

We'll begin by looking in more depth at hourly rates—not the specific dollar figure you should charge but the usefulness and disadvantages of this method of pricing. Then we'll take a quick look at project rates, a subject discussed in much more detail later. We'll examine two other pricing strategies that can be used by independent contractors in virtually any line of work: per diem rates and retainers. We'll also consider a number of other pricing methods that are used less frequently but should not be overlooked, because they may be excellent options in certain situations.

## Hourly Rates

Many self-employed service providers charge by the hour, whether they are $15-an-hour typists for hire or $150-an-hour accountants. The great advantage of this method of pricing is that the longer you work, the more you earn. With some other pricing methods, such as project rates and retainers, the fee remains the same whether you take five hours or fifty hours to complete the job. With hourly fees, on the other hand, someone who takes ten times as long as a faster colleague to do the work will earn ten times as much as the speed demon.

If you operate best at a slow, steady pace, hourly fees may be your best pricing strategy. But if you are quick, your total earnings on a project will be less than those of a poky competitor charging the same hourly rate. Should you be penalized for doing a good job fast?

Alice, Barbara, and Carol all charge $40 an hour for their freelance services. Alice completes a job in five hours and bills $200. Barbara completes a comparable job in seven hours and bills $280. Like Alice, Carol takes five hours to do the same work. But her invoice states that she logged six hours on the job, and she charges $240.

Carol has padded her bill. Knowing that she works fast, she routinely augments her actual hours on a job by 20 percent. She does not feel that she should be punished for doing a good job quickly, and she finds that padding is the only way to make hourly fees work for her. Carol's clients have never complained that her bills are too high, and they continue to send new work her way.

Dan also pads his bills—when he can. Many of his clients insist that he work on their premises. But if he goes to a client's office four days from 9:00 A.M. to 5:00 P.M., his invoice cannot indicate that he worked forty hours. Padding works only when Big Brother is not watching.

Rather than pad his bills, Emilio decided to compensate for his efficient work pace by setting his hourly rate very high. Clients he has worked for know that his final bill will be reasonable, and they continue to call him. He feels that he has probably lost potential new clients, however, because they have been frightened off by his high fee.

Some clients are reluctant to hire an independent contractor who wants to be paid by the hour, regardless of how reasonable the rate may be. A tightly budgeted client might be anxious about the unknown: how many hours it will take to complete the job. Such clients often prefer that consultants work for a flat fee or a project rate.

## Project Rates

Clients like project rates because they reveal in advance exactly what to allocate in the budget for a particular job. The Internal Revenue Service also is less likely to question whether someone is an independent contractor (rather than an employee, for whom the company should be deducting taxes) when payment is on a project basis.

For the consultant, a project rate can be the best choice—or the worst one. The problem with project rates is that you have to commit in advance to a fixed fee, often before you know much about the job. If you set the rate high enough to cover all unforeseen disasters, the result can be more than satisfactory. On the other hand, if you agree to do a job for a flat fee and the project then turns out to be bigger than you were first led to believe, the return can be horrendous.

Consider the experiences of Frank and George, freelancers who were hired for the same project. After the client discussed

# Can you charge for travel time?
# If so, do you bill it at your usual rate?

Travel can be divided into two categories: local commuting and out-of-town trips. What applies to the first category doesn't necessarily hold for the second.

Billing for local travel time is an issue mainly when you're charging by the hour. Some consultants assess a lower rate, such as half their hourly fee, for the time it takes to go between their own office and their client's. But some freelancers, reasoning that they are unable to work for other clients while commuting, charge their full hourly fee. Still other consultants ignore travel time, especially if it is not substantial. No matter which option you select, do not itemize travel time on your invoices. Your client does not need to know that you are billing for the commute, especially if you are charging less than your customary hourly fee. However, if your commute involves expensive train or bus rides or tolls, you might arrange for reimbursement upon submission of transit receipts.

When billing by a method other than an hourly fee, such as a project rate or unit price, allow for commuting when you calculate your fee. Be sure to account for the time you expect to be on the road if the distance between your office and your client's is considerable or

the job individually with them, she asked each for a project rate. Frank quoted $10,000, George $8,000. As it turned out, Frank's part of the project was easier than he had anticipated and he was able to complete it in 120 hours. Thus, his hourly earnings amounted to $83.33. However, George's part of the project mushroomed beyond his expectations and it took him twice as long as Frank: 240 hours. Because he had agreed to a project rate of $8,000, his hourly take was just $33.33.

if you anticipate many trips. Also, include the costs of the commute in your projected expenses when calculating a flat fee.

A client who sends you out of town should cover your costs in one way or another. You could submit an expense reimbursement form at the end of your trip, or ask the client to handle the travel arrangements so that the bills are sent directly to the company. If the client is reluctant to pay for the trip, incorporate the costs into your fee, either by calculating them into a flat rate or by converting them to equivalent hourly charges. For example, add ten hours to your bill if you incur $300 in travel expenses and work for $30 an hour.

You should also expect compensation for the time you are out of town on business. Consider these choices:

- Charge a per diem fee for each day away from your office.

- Include the anticipated out-of-town time as you tally the hours when setting a project rate.

- When billing by the hour, assess your full fee for every hour you work on the road and at least half your usual fee for the time you are in transit.

Did George set his project rate too low? Did he underestimate how long the job would take? Should he have left himself some leeway for renegotiating if the project took a different turn than anticipated? In fact, any of these oversights might have made this a money-losing job for George. Because these problems are so common—and because project rates have the potential to be very rewarding, as Frank discovered—project rates will be examined in detail later.

## Per Diem Rates

A different type of flat fee is a fixed rate per day, or a per diem. This payment method is used by consultants in many fields.

The main problem with a per diem is that the consultant and the client have to agree in advance on the definition of a day. Is it a typical eight-hour work day? Or twenty-four hours? Or even until the job is done?

Hillary's regular per diem rate is $350. A client agreed to pay her per diem rate for the four days that she would be working on the job. The job would be in Hillary's hands on Monday and had to be delivered before a meeting on Friday morning.

Hillary received the material on Monday at 2:00 P.M. and worked until midnight that day, then from 9:00 A.M. to 10:00 P.M. Tuesday, from 9:00 A.M. to 6:00 P.M. Wednesday (she had made plans for the evening long ago), and from 8:00 A.M. to 11:00 P.M. Thursday. Without subtracting time for intervening activities, like eating, Hillary logged 45 hours on this job (not including the time for the Friday morning delivery). That made her hourly earnings about $31, versus the $45 to $53 she normally expects to make with her $350 per diem. Assuming that she took off two hours a day for meals, phone calls, and other run-of-the-mill activities, she barely earned $40 an hour—considerably less than what she expects from her per diem.

Personally, I dislike the per diem method of pay and almost never use it. The exception I make is for meetings, especially out-of-town affairs. Traveling wastes a lot of time, time that cannot be spent working for other clients. Yet out-of-town meetings also require a consultant to perform during time that is not necessarily billable. For example, when sharing a cab to the airport you might chat about business. A per diem rate allows you to earn some compensation under these circumstances.

## Retainers

If you have developed an ongoing relationship with a client, you might want to work out a retainer. A retainer is a fixed sum that a client pays a consultant on a regular basis, usually monthly or annually. The payment period could also be based on a regularly scheduled project, such as a quarterly audit. In return for the retainer, the consultant promises to be available at the client's request.

A retainer works best if the consultant does the same work in each payment period. It may also make sense if a slim workload in one payment period is balanced by a heavy amount in another. Retainers can be poor arrangements, however, if the work to be done is unpredictable.

Jim, Jane, and John each receive $250 a month on a retainer basis. Jim's job is to proofread a newsletter. Because the newsletter is always the same length and the amount of work is similar for each issue, the retainer translates every month into nearly the same earnings for each hour Jim works. Jane's retainer is for updating a Web site. When few changes are required, she might work on the site only one or two hours a month. When the client has a lot to share electronically, she might spend ten or fifteen hours updating the site. Over the course of a year, Jane averages five hours a month working for this client. She is satisfied with her average earnings of $50 an hour, which comes on top of the much greater fee she originally garnered for developing the Web site.

John, however, has not had good luck with his retainer. His client calls him constantly, and he spends at least two hours every week working for him. Although two hours may not seem like a lot of time, this client thinks that because John is on a retainer he should stop everything else and respond to his requests immediately. John puts in at least eight hours a month for this client, and sometimes as many as twenty-five hours. In addition, he risks alienating other clients because of the demands of his retainer business.

Some consultants like the idea of a retainer because it assures them a certain base income. If you do decide to go after a retainer, be sure you know the client well and can predict with some accuracy the amount of work involved. You don't want to find yourself in John's shoes, with a demanding client who has an erratic workload. An uneven work flow by itself is not necessarily bad, as Jane discovered, provided that it balances out over the long run to be a satisfactory expenditure of your time.

Another word of caution about retainers: They shouldn't represent too great a portion of your income. Suppose a client pays you a retainer of $1,000 a month, which represents one third of your total annual income. Because of the time you devote to this business, you can work for only a few other clients. In such a situation the Internal Revenue Service may question whether you are truly an independent contractor or are actually an employee of your retainer client. This could have important implications at tax time.

## Unit Pricing

When you go to the store, whether to buy a loaf of bread or a ream of paper, you pay by the unit. Entrepreneurs who create and sell products probably will choose unit pricing as their main method of charging. Some self-employed people who provide services may also opt for unit pricing. An attorney may assess a standard rate for an uncomplicated will, for example, and a freelance photographer might charge a flat fee per picture.

In addition, unit pricing may be the way to go when a project consists of discrete items that require a similar amount of work. In essence, each unit can be considered a mini-project, so in this respect you could think of unit pricing as a variation on project rates.

Kate uses database and desktop publishing software to create directories. Each directory listing entails similar work—entering information into a database, proofreading it at several stages, and converting it to a standard printed format for the finished book. Kate charges a fixed fee per unit, that is, for each directory listing. She likes this pricing strategy because her income goes up as the number of listings increases.

At one time, Kate charged a flat fee to produce an entire directory, basing her project rate on the anticipated number of entries. Then she learned that this was not necessarily a wise strategy when she agreed to a flat project fee for a directory that was expected to contain 500 listings. By the time the project was done, it held 700 listings. When Kate got burned on that project, she vowed to switch to unit pricing for all future directories. Now if a directory has 700 listings, she earns 700 times her unit rate.

## Percentage Take

The best-known version of pricing according to percentage earnings comes from the world of sales. There the percentage goes by a different name: the commission.

Entrepreneurs in fields other than sales can try several takes on the percentage concept. Stuart, a professional fund-raiser, believes that the best way to inspire clients' confidence is to work on a percentage basis. He charges a small up-front flat fee and later bills so many cents for every dollar that his campaign attracts. Stuart has many clients, who reason that a consultant self-assured enough to risk income on results must be extremely capable.

Grant writers also use a variety of percentage pricing. A grant might stipulate that a consultant will earn a certain percentage of the total endowment. This is a less risky percentage take than the portion-of-business payment of the sales and fund-raising professionals. Once the grant is awarded, the consultant knows how much money will be going to the bank.

## Head-count Fees

A consultant who sells a service usually does not care how many people use that service. Every now and then, though, the number of partakers can figure into the pricing equation. A corporate trainer, for example, often charges a set fee for each participant in a training program. Such a head-count fee may be in addition to a base fee for the course or could be the sole method of pricing.

Larry and Linda combine their computer expertise and teaching skills to give their own computer courses. Larry targets large corporations, Linda individuals who want to be better able to meet the technological challenges of the twenty-first century. To assure personal attention yet take advantage of group interaction, they both like classes of five people. Larry charges his corporate clients a base fee of $400 per ninety-minute session, plus $50 per person per class. Linda charges each student $130 a session. When five people attend one of their training programs, Larry and Linda both earn $650 per class.

## Page and Word Rates

Writers are often paid by the page or by the word. The client, not the freelancer, sets the rate, making these methods unlike the other pricing strategies that we have considered. Surprisingly, the main caveat regarding the page-rate method of payment is the definition of a page. Most writers assume that it is a double-spaced typed page, which usually translates into 250 words. But if the client considers a page to be a single-spaced sheet of paper, the writer will earn only half as much as anticipated. A publisher could instruct its freelancers to use narrow margins and small type fonts, in effect squeezing 350 words onto a page.

The lesson here is clear. If you agree to work at a client's rate, be sure you are speaking the same language. Even something as simple as a page can take on many meanings. (How long, for instance, is a Web page?)

The same caveat applies with word rates: Know what the client means by this seemingly innocuous term. A word is a word, right? Right, but a phrase in Russian does not contain the same number of words as its English equivalent. If you are a freelance translator being paid by the word, be sure to ask whether this is a word in the language of origin or in the target language.

## Mix and Match

Clearly, you have a number of options for pricing. You probably will not stick with one method exclusively, although you may prefer one over all the others. Depending on the circumstances, though, be daring and try a different pricing strategy if you think it will help you come out ahead.

Is it fair to charge differently for different customers? Of course. Large manufacturing corporations do this all the time, setting a base price and then offering discounts to large-volume purchasers. Some companies may also charge less for the little guy or for nonprofit organizations and government agencies. Sale events lower prices. Special attention, such as overnight shipping or overseas distribution, jacks up the price. If big producers of goods can vary their prices, so can you. Not only can you vary your charges; you can also be flexible in the methods you use to determine them.

At times you may want to mix strategies for a particular assignment. For example, you could charge by the hour except for days when you have to attend meetings, assessing a per diem rate on those occasions. Or you could work by the hour until you know enough about a job to determine a project rate.

Remember Jim, who received a $250-a-month retainer for proofreading a newsletter? When his client asked him to proofread the annual index, he said he would have to bill separately for that because it was beyond the usual scope covered by the retainer. When the client agreed that this was reasonable, Jim charged an hourly fee for proofing the index.

## Hourly Rates as the Common Denominator

Throughout this chapter, while exploring alternatives to hourly rates, earnings per hour have continued to crop up. Frank assessed a flat fee of $10,000, logged 120 hours, and in effect earned $83.33 per hour. George worked 240 hours for a flat fee of $8,000, netting $33.33 an hour. Hillary's $350 per diem for a four-day project translated into $31 to $40 an hour. Jane's $250-a-month retainer averaged $50 an hour. If these consultants were not charging by the hour, why bother to calculate their hourly earnings?

Converting your income into hourly earnings, no matter what your actual method of pricing, offers a good basis for comparison. Otherwise, you'll be comparing apples and oranges when you try to determine what works best for you. If you convert all prices into their hourly rate equivalents, you'll ensure that you're looking only at apples. You may have Granny Smiths and Jonathans and Golden Delicious, but at least they'll all be apples.

It's easy to convert your earnings on any assignment into the hourly rate equivalent. Just subtract your expenses from your total income, then divide the result by the hours logged on the job. The equation follows:

> Hourly Rate Equivalent =
> (Total Income – Expenses) ÷ Hours Logged

Determining your hourly rate equivalent for each job has several advantages:

- It's hard to evaluate your pricing strategies if you look only at your total take. Changing your earnings to an hourly rate shows how much actual effort you needed to attain that income.

- As we'll see later, one way to determine project rates—perhaps the best way—is to multiply the hours that you anticipate the job will take by the amount that you would like to earn per hour. Conversely, dividing your project fee by the hours actually logged reveals your accuracy in estimating how long the job would take. You may discover that you need to hone your estimating skills.

- When you work for a client who determines the rates rather than lets you set the fee, converting your earnings into hourly income helps you decide whether the client is paying you enough for the amount of effort you are expending.

After converting his pay into hourly income, Oliver, a freelance writer, discovered that a client he thought was stingy was actually a moneymaker for him, whereas a client he thought was generous was in fact a losing proposition. Both clients paid by the page, one offering $50 per double-spaced page and the other $100 for the same number of words. Because the nature of the work was different, Oliver could produce a $50 page in one hour, whereas it took him three hours to complete a $100 page. Although he earned twice as much per page from the latter client, he had to work three times as long to churn out the work. In the end, the $50-a-page client was a $50-an-hour deal; the $100-a-page client netted only $33.33 an hour. Oliver decided to drop the $100-a-page client and to take more work from the $50-a-page publisher.

# 3

# Log Logic

I HADN'T seen much of my friend Paul, a freelance architect, all summer. He was consumed by a major project and was working day and night, through weekends and holidays. The day his client gave the final okay on his drawings, after numerous redesigns, we met for dinner.

"Was it worth it?" I asked.

"I guess. I made $20,000 for this phase. Not bad for a summer of hell."

"You must have logged hundreds of hours on that job," I ventured.

"I suppose," Paul said. "I don't keep track of my hours when I'm paid a flat fee."

Later I sat down with a calculator and played with some numbers. Suppose Paul had worked 50 hours a week for the 12 weeks of summer. That would be a total of 600 hours logged on the job. He had earned $20,000. His hourly rate equivalent (20,000 ÷ 600) was $33.33. That's not very much for someone with Paul's talents and experience.

Like Paul, many freelancers don't keep track of their time if they're charging by some method other than an hourly rate. In fact, some consultants prefer nonhourly methods of pay not because they are more profitable, but because they don't involve as much record keeping. "I dislike charging by the hour, because I can't be bothered keeping track of my time," more than one independent contractor has told me.

On the other hand, some consultants become obsessive about logging their hours. Roberta keeps a multicolored diary, blocking out the hours she devotes to her consulting business in blue, the time she volunteers for her children's schools in red, and her exercise periods in green. "All of these things are important to me," she explains. "I want to see lots of each color every week."

Richard also keeps a multicolored log, but his is reserved for business. He works for about ten clients each year and assigns a different-colored pencil to each. Sun's logbook is not color coded but, like Roberta's and Richard's logs, it meticulously accounts for every minute of her day. Sam, who can't remember life before computers, keeps his records in an electronic calendar program on his hard drive as well as in his palm-top unit.

Each of these detailed logs tells when the record keeper was at work. The logs indicate how much to bill when charging by the hour. In addition, Roberta can review her weekly diary to see how well she is balancing three important areas of her life. Richard can tell at a glance how many clients he has worked for in any given period. Sun and Sam see the pattern of their workdays. These logs reveal a great deal about the entrepreneurs' work habits, but they do not actually provide much useful information for managing or improving the business.

If you are going to keep track of your time on the job—and everyone should—why not keep records that will give you data you can put to practical uses? The most valuable logs are those that record not just the hours you worked but what you were doing during that time. In other words, what tasks did you need to perform to complete your assignment?

## Task Master

Every job consists of a series of tasks. Even a seemingly simple job can be broken down into its component tasks. For example,

Vivian is a freelance word processor. During the course of an assignment she may do the following:

- Scan the raw material to see what style elements it contains (subheads, lists, etc.)

- Make formatting decisions regarding the various style elements

- Type the material

- Print it out

- Proof it

- Make corrections

- Write a memo to the client

- Prepare the final package, with printout, disk, memo, invoice, etc.

- Deliver the material to the client.

Rather than simply log "noon–5:30 P.M." as the time spent working on a twenty-five-page document, Vivian notes how long it took her to do each task. How many of these five and a half hours were actually spent typing? How long did it take to proof the twenty-five pages? What else did she have to do as part of this job?

It's easy to keep a task log. Just take a piece of paper or a page in your logbook, or, if you are not computer phobic, set up a database. Note each task you do and how long you spend on it. Include other information that will help you calculate your average speed in completing particular tasks.

Vivian's log sheet for typing that twenty-five–page paper is presented as Figure 1 (page 24). The numbers on the right of the log are the time it took her to do each task. She records her time to the nearest quarter-hour. This is a convenient method, although sticklers for detail may prefer to log by the minute. If a job extends over several days, Vivian erases the time recorded on revisited tasks and substitutes the sum of the hours logged previously

**Figure 1**
**Log Sheet for Typing a Twenty-Five–Page Paper**

| | |
|---|---|
| Look over material, decide on style | ¼ hr. |
| Type (25 pp.) | 2½ |
| Proof | 2 |
| Make corrections, run final printout | ¾ |
| **Total** | 5½ hrs. |

plus those worked on the new day. Record keepers who don't like to erase might set up a different time column for each day and total the columns at the end of a job.

A task-oriented log helps Vivian make business decisions and charge appropriate fees. Besides telling her how much to charge when billing by the hour, this type of log reveals:

- How many pages Vivian can type in an hour

- How many pages she can proof an hour

- How much time besides the actual typing time she needs to allow for a job

- How much more work she can accept, given her current workload

- Whether the client has realistic expectations about how long the job should take

- What to charge as a flat fee when she sets a price for other jobs

- Whether the price a client quotes her is fair for a given job

- Whether a job she has completed at a fixed fee the client set turned out to be a good deal

Let's see how information from her logs can help Vivian with other projects. From the job described earlier and other work she has logged in the past, she knows she can type about ten to twelve pages an hour if she is given neat material. If she is working from handwritten copy or transcribing a tape, she averages eight to ten pages an hour. She can proof her work at her fastest typing speed, ten to twelve pages an hour. Vivian also knows that no matter what the assignment, she needs to allow time for general administration, such as preparing the final printout, disk, and invoice.

Suppose a client asks Vivian to take on a 200-page assignment, which must be completed in four days. He says she'll be given a heavily edited document, without a disk. Assuming a worst-case scenario, Vivian calculates that she can type only eight pages an hour, which means she'll need twenty-five hours for the typing alone. It will take another twenty hours to proof the job at the rate of ten pages an hour. For these two tasks together she may need as much as forty-five hours. That's more than eleven hours a day, not including "general administration" time. The total project could come closer to forty-eight or fifty hours.

Vivian tells her client that she cannot do the job in four days. He offers to give her an extra day, or even as much as a day and a half if it will help. Even so, she still could be facing long stretches at the keyboard. But this good client is a regular customer and she would like to accommodate him. So she offers two compromises:

- She'll do the job in four days at her usual rate of $20 an hour, but it won't be proofed.

- She'll return it neatly typed and fully proofed in five days or early on day six, but she will charge $25 an hour as a rush fee.

Because the client needs a perfect, mistake-free document, he agrees to the rush surcharge.

As it turns out, Vivian logs a total of fifty-one hours—and a lot of back and neck strain. At $25 an hour she earns $1,275. She would have earned $1,020 if she had charged her usual rate of $20, so she came out $255 ahead. (She used some of the rush-fee bonus to pay for a massage for her sore muscles.)

Because she kept task-oriented logs, Vivian knew that her client had underestimated how long the job would take. Armed with this knowledge, she felt confident asking for either a more manageable assignment or a higher fee than usual. Unlike the architect Paul, whose failure to keep good records caused him to guess how well he was doing, Vivian *knew* what she needed to do to bring home decent pay for a grueling week.

## Taking the Sting out of Poison Ivy

Vivian's log sheet listed only a few tasks. More complicated jobs entail more tasks, and their log sheets are therefore longer. But no matter how many tasks are involved, the time it takes to prepare a log sheet is minimal. Just make a note of the task and check your watch when you begin and end it. We'll discuss later in this chapter how accurate your clock needs to be.

Figure 2 shows a longer project log from my own files. The job was to write an article about poison ivy, based on interviews with three experts on the subject. After the client approved a detailed outline, which I wrote based on background reading, I conducted and recorded interviews. The client transcribed the tapes, and after reviewing the transcripts, I was ready to start writing.

Like Vivian, I record my time on each task to the nearest quarter-hour. The numbers in parentheses contain information I can use to calculate averages. For example, I conducted three interviews, which averaged an hour each, and prepared four tables and figure legends. I record expenses on the bottom of the log sheet, so I can find costs easily when I calculate the hourly rate equivalent.

I kept this detailed log sheet even though I was being paid by the page, not the hour. The amount of time it took to write the article would not affect my pay, nor would the hours logged on each specific task. So why keep such a record?

## More Than Numbers

A task-oriented log gives a consultant a wealth of information about his or her own work and helps in pricing future jobs. Logs I have kept over the years have offered me the following insights:

**Figure 2**
**Log Sheet for Writing an Article on Poison Ivy**

| | |
|---|---|
| Background reading | 4 hrs. |
| Prepare outline | 3½ |
| Discuss with client | ¾ |
| Correspond with experts | 2¼ |
| Conduct interviews (3) | 3 |
| Review transcripts (3) | 2¾ |
| | |
| Draft main article (12 pp.) | 7 |
| Write tables and figure legends (4) | 1¾ |
| Write sidebars (2) | 2½ |
| Edit material on paper (18 pp.) | 4¾ |
| Edit on disk | 1½ |
| | |
| General administration | 1¼ |
| | |
| **Total** | 35 hrs. |
| | |
| Long-distance calls | $45 |
| Postage, including express service | $27 |

- Task logs remind me what a job entails. Writing is not just writing. The items above the gap about halfway down the task list for the poison ivy article represent all the work that occurs before I put a word on paper. I have to assume that I could spend as much time preparing to write as I do actually writing. It is essential to keep this preparatory time in mind when pricing a job.

- With task logs, personal work patterns become clear. A pattern I once discovered was that it usually took me about half as long to edit a draft as to write it. The pattern held for years, then suddenly it changed. I started to take as long to edit as to write, sometimes even longer. The discovery of this change in a long-established work pattern caused me to delve into the causes and address the underlying inefficiencies in my recent work style.

- Knowing my work patterns helps me schedule my assignment load. I can accept or reject a new job based in part on how much time I must allow for the work already on my desk.

- The accuracy of a client's time or money estimate can be assessed from past project logs. When one client expected me to edit a 600-page manuscript within three weeks, I consulted logs from other editing jobs and saw that I needed at least twice as much time, given my previous commitments. I turned down the job. Not long afterward, the same client asked me to write an article from the transcript of a lecture for a fee of $200. I was earning $300 to $450 from other clients to write articles of similar length and complexity, using tapes rather than transcripts. After checking my project logs for the latter articles to learn how much time was related to using the tapes, I calculated that the rate for the transcript-based article was too low. When I presented my case to the client, he raised the fee to $300—not just for this one article but for all future work, and not just for me but for all freelancers on similar assignments.

- Project logs can help determine an appropriate per diem. I base my per diem in part on what I can most likely accomplish in seven hours—but also on the possibility of a ten-hour day.

- Now for the most important reason to keep task-oriented time logs: the best project rates are based on estimates of the number of hours each component task will take. When I am asked to estimate the price for a project, I review past log sheets to see how long I needed to complete similar tasks for other jobs. Using time estimates based on comparable experience from my own files, I can come up with reasonable expectations of the number of hours the job will take. I use this time estimate to calculate the project fee. This process is discussed in much more detail in Chapters 6 and 7.

My log sheets, handwritten on lined yellow paper, reside in the work folder for each project. They are the second item in the folder once the project is completed; the invoice goes on top. I can easily retrieve them if I want data to estimate prices for new jobs.

If, like Roberta, you want to see at a glance how you are balancing your life, continue to keep records to suit those needs. But also maintain task-oriented logs for each job. Keep this type of detailed log for every project, no matter how you are being paid: by the hour, on a per diem basis, as a flat project fee, on retainer, or by some other method.

## Stop the Clock!

Many consultants confess that they don't like to keep detailed time sheets because they're confused about when they should stop the clock. When interruptions occur—the telephone rings, you need to put paper in the printer, or you have to go to the bathroom or get a drink of water—should you turn off the clock?

Elaborate arguments can be and are made pro and con. The reason consultants most often cite to keep the clock running is that just as staff employees are not docked for telephone or bathroom time, neither should consultants be expected to work without interruption. In my field of publishing, freelancers have developed fancy names for clocking their time, including "stopwatch editing" and the "editorial hour" (48 minutes on the clock being seen as equivalent to one hour of billable time, to allow for unavoidable interruptions, according to one fellow freelancer).

Interesting though these discussions may be, they are dwelling on the wrong point. Whether or not you're billing by the hour, your time sheet should give you more information than how long you worked, with or without interruptions. Your records don't have to state how long an hour is and when you stopped the clock. But they should tell you what you can accomplish in an hour of work. Once you start logging by task, you'll stop focusing on how many minutes of working time are in an hour and start to comprehend what you can in fact do in an hour's time.

When you make this shift, you'll probably find that you round up your time (like the 48-minute "editorial hour"). The reason is not the interruptions that break your concentration. Rather, you'll round up your hours because when you refer to your logs later to price a job or to evaluate a client's estimate, you'll want a realistic figure, not an ideal situation. It's always best to assume that a job will take longer than the ideal.

## Try It; You'll Like It

When I have give workshops on pricing for freelance editors and writers, nearly everyone comments favorably on their evaluation forms about the logic of logging by task:

- "It's the most practical approach to record keeping I've ever heard."

- "I'm going to start logging by task immediately."

- "This will help me see clearly what it is I do when I work."

Years after taking my workshop, freelancers have told me that the most important advice they ever received in their self-employment careers was to log their time according to the tasks involved. You can verify this for yourself. For six months, keep task-oriented logs on every project you do, whether you are paid by the hour, the day, the job, or whatever. After you've used the information in your logs to price other jobs and to manage your business better, you should be convinced that the little bit of record-keeping effort was worth it.

# 4

# Going After the Going Rate

IN D. L. COBURN's Pulitzer Prize–winning play *The Gin Game*, the elderly Weller Martin recalls his early days as a marketing consultant. At one point he had desperately wanted a particular job and thought he could probably get $500 for it. He was feeling anxious, however, about asking that much. When the client asked him how much the job was going to cost, the nervous Weller stammered, "Four."

"Four thousand?" the boss replied. "Yeah, that sounds about right to me."

The person to whom Weller is relating this story then asks if he told the boss he actually meant $400, since that was closer to what he had first thought the job was worth.

Weller replies, "It was worth whatever he was willing to pay."

Weller Martin had learned an important lesson: When pricing a job, go with what the market will bear. He was lucky to have found out with little effort what the market would bear for this particular assignment. It's not always so easy to learn the going rate.

31

## Why Do You Have to Be Like Everyone Else?

Suppose Weller had been able to muster more than a single syllable and had stated that he wanted $400 for the job. The client probably would have given him a puzzled look and said, "Let me think about it. I'll call you in a few days." Weller would then have sat by the phone in vain while the client looked for another marketing consultant, one who had sized up the job well enough to know that it was worth thousands of dollars, not hundreds.

Clients generally prefer to deal with people who charge within the range of typical rates. They may be reluctant to hire someone whose fees are substantially lower than average, suspecting that this particular independent contractor is not a professional. On the other hand, clients may turn down a high bidder, knowing that they can choose from a pool of freelancers who offer similar services for substantially less.

Experienced consultants and clients alike know that typical rate ranges are quite wide for most types of work. Even within a narrow specialty, the going rate can cover a broad swath.

In 1996, in preparation for a talk to the New York chapter of the American Medical Writers Association (AMWA), members of that organization were asked to complete a brief questionnaire reporting the fees that they charge for six specified types of projects. Ten people indicated their fees for writing a 20-minute video script. The range was between $2,500 and $7,500, with six of the ten script writers charging between $3,000 and $5,000. In other words, some New York medical video script writers charge two or three times as much as their lowest-priced colleagues. What's more, the "average" fee for this highly specialized work performed by professionals in a narrow geographic locale covers a $2,000 span.

### Refining the Market

If the survey had covered all the video script writers across the country, not just New York medical writers, the range of rates would have been even broader. A number of factors can affect what the market will bear:

- *The part of the country.* Earnings—whether for freelancers or for staff employees—generally tend to be lowest in the South and the interior of the country, highest in the Northeast and the West Coast. There are exceptions, of course. A concentration or a dearth of specialists in a given region can raise the fees for all consultants performing related work in a particular locale.

- *The segment of the industry.* Nonprofit organizations tend to pay less than *Fortune* 500 companies. Government agencies are known to inflate the bank accounts of independent contractors, although small municipalities may have limited budgets for consultants. Individuals who engage the services of consultants generally offer less money than large corporations.

- *The time allotted.* Freelancers may be expected to work all hours of the day and night until the job is done. But a generous client with an impossible deadline might be willing to pay more for rush work.

- *The special background needed for a job.* An assignment that requires special skills or knowledge should pay more than one that anyone could do. A multinational corporation seeking a consultant with contacts in Japan who speaks and writes the language and is well versed in import-export laws should expect to pay well for someone with this combination of skills.

When we talk about what the market will bear, therefore, we are not speaking of a stable entity. "The market" is a chameleon capable of change at any moment. Astute consultants alter their fees as the market changes its colors.

Diane, an independent researcher, is hired by people hungry for information who do not have the time or wherewithal to delve into a subject themselves. Her clients range from individuals seeking information about their ancestors to multinational companies wanting in-depth profiles of their competition. Diane would price her services beyond the means of individual clients if

she charged them as much as she assesses her corporate customers, and she would not make a livable income if she charged corporate clients what individual information seekers can afford. Her
fees differ greatly for these ends of her client spectrum, as do the
products she delivers. Her research is thorough no matter who is
paying the bill. But the individual who pays $150 gets a small
report, rarely more than five pages summarizing the highlights
of the research, whereas the corporation that pays $7,000 re-
ceives a thirty- to forty-page analysis of the findings.

   The president of a company for whom Diane had done research asked her to carry out some personal fact finding for him.
Diane knew he could afford to pay more than her typical individual client. He also was accustomed to paying her corporate
rates. Knowing that the market could bear a lot in this case, Diane
charged a high fee. Her research report was the detailed type of
analysis that the company president had come to expect of her.
He felt that he had received his money's worth, and Diane was
happy with her earnings.

   Diane knew what to charge in this case because she was familiar
with the client. But what if you're dealing with an unknown? How do
you determine the going rate? There are two ways to learn what the
market will bear: ask the competition, and ask the client.

## Learning from Your Colleagues

I don't like to think of people who do my type of work as competition. I prefer to think of them as colleagues. In the us-versus-
them world, the enemy is not the people like ourselves but those
on the other side of the assignment desk: the clients.

   Because I maintain that we entrepreneurs are all in this together, I have no trouble asking other freelancers what they charge
for particular types of work. Similarly, my fellow medical writers
and editors know that if they ask me, I will willingly talk money
with them. Not everyone is so open about sharing pricing information, however. When you call your colleagues to learn the going rate for an upcoming job, you might try one of these
conversation starters:

- "I'm talking to a client about [type of job]. Have you done anything like this recently?" [After loosening up the consultant, add the next line.] "Would you mind telling me what you got?"

- "I have the possibility of [describe work]. Do you know what the typical rates are for this kind of job?"

- "A client has asked me to do [type of work]. Do you know anyone who's done this sort of job who might be willing to talk to me, especially about rates?"

- "I'm supposed to call a client tomorrow with a bid for [describe job]. I was thinking of asking [fee]. Do you think this is reasonable?"

- "A client approached me about doing [type of work]. Do you have any pricing suggestions?"

Sharing information with others in the field is an age-old activity with a contemporary name: networking. Thanks to computers, networks spread far and fast. Take advantage of cyberspace to augment working the phone and learn what the market will bear.

Alex, a freelance computer programmer who lives in St. Louis, has become online friends with Meg, an independent programmer who lives in Chicago. When Alex, who usually works for nonprofit organizations, was approached by a large company to restructure its database, he asked Meg if she thought his usual fee was too low for this client. She encouraged him to raise his rate, and the client agreed to the fee without an argument. Meanwhile, when Meg took an assignment from the local branch of a company based in Boston, Alex gave her the e-mail address of a Boston friend, who told her the going rate for programming in his part of the country. Because her fee was being paid out of corporate headquarters, she asked for more than she normally charges—and got it.

You may have skimmed this section, protesting, "This won't work for me. Nobody else does the kind of work I do." Most of us are probably not as unique as we might like to think, however. Even if you provide one-of-a-kind services, another consultant offers similar services, albeit not as specialized as yours. That person may have valuable pricing information to share, if only you could make contact.

How do you identify other consultants in your own or a related line of work? The modern way is to surf the Internet, starting with a word such as *consultant* or the name of your specialty. That's how Alex and Meg became friends. If you prefer to do your research on the ground rather than in cyberspace, go to the library and check the *Encyclopedia of Associations*, as well as telephone directories of major cities, for organizations of interest. A brief list of organizations made up of independent professionals appears in the Appendix.

If you are not already affiliated with an organization for people in your line of work, you ought to consider joining one. Professional associations are an excellent way to connect with like-minded entrepreneurs whom you can call upon when you need business advice. In addition, professional organizations sometimes conduct formal or informal rates surveys, like the one described earlier for AMWA. Although organizations may share results of rates surveys with outsiders, such information is more likely reserved for members only.

Both personal contact with fellow members of a professional association and use of the group's rates survey have advantages. Checking the results of a survey saves time. The ten medical video script writers were only one-fourth of the AMWA survey respondents, and the forty people who took the time to complete the survey were just a small fraction of the total membership. It could take 200 phone calls to find ten people who write scripts for medical videos and are willing to share pricing information. Yet personal chats with others in the field will likely yield useful nuggets that a survey form cannot gather.

## Persuading a Client to Spill the Beans

Clients can be surprisingly reticent about revealing the going rate for a job. We've all been down this road. After describing a job, the client asks, "How much will you charge?" The consultant responds, "What did you have in mind?" The client retorts, "I'd rather you give me a figure, and I'll let you know if that will work out." When the consultant quotes a number, the client responds, "That's much more than we had in mind!"

This jousting could be avoided if clients were not so anxious to save a buck. They play this game hoping the consultant will suggest a lower figure than they have budgeted. The client in fact knows what is an acceptable rate but hopes the contractor will be content with less.

Try the following approaches with clients who are reluctant to be the first to blink. In doing so you are essentially asking the question, "What are you willing to pay?" but couching it in different terms.

- Ask the client for a range of acceptable rates, rather than a single figure.

- Ask if the client has a set rate or range for other freelancers. You might explain, "My background and the work you want me to do may be different. But knowing the pay scale for your other freelancers will help me understand what rates you think are fair."

- Ask the client, "What is your budget?" You might be given the figure for the overall project, not just your small piece of the pie. But at least you'll have some numbers to work with. And you might then consider bidding on more of the project.

- Be a bit outrageous and challenge the client with rates you feel are unreasonable.

The last suggestion is how Harvey, a freelance copy editor, made a killing working for the notoriously low-paying publishing industry. A publisher needed a copy editor for a large, multiauthored book. Harvey told him, "It sounds like a project I would like to do. But I have to be honest with you. If you're willing to pay only $2,000 or $3,000, there's no point in continuing this discussion."

"Oh, no," the publisher replied, "we intend to pay more than that. However, one freelancer wanted to charge $8,500, and we think that's much too high." Now Harvey knew the budget: more than $3,000 but less than $8,500.

# Can you charge extra for overtime or rush work?

Freelancers are often engaged because clients assume that they can work long into the night or on weekends if necessary. "Overtime pay" is not a term in most clients' vocabularies when talking about freelancers. But working more than 40 hours a week (the usual overtime trigger for wage earners) is a different matter than doing 40 hours' worth of work in three days. In the latter case, a consultant who is being asked to cram an impossible task into no time flat may be able to assess a rush fee.

Semantics aside, you can in fact charge a higher fee than usual without calling it an overtime or rush rate. How you earn more depends on your billing method.

## Topping the Going Rate

Although you will usually want to ask for a fee within the broad range of going rates, there may be times when your price is more than the highest rate you have heard or less than the lowest-earning consultants charge. These are the most common reasons to ask for more than the competition is receiving:

- *You suspect that the client has not told you everything about a job.* Far too often, clients insist on a quote before they have given enough information on which to base the bid. The demand for a premature commitment is not necessarily related to a desire to save a dollar. The client simply may not know everything about a job. Chapter 5 explains how to garner as much information as possible before you name your price. If you have reason to believe the job may be more complex than the client suggests, you may want to charge top dollar.

- If you're billing by the day, make your per diem fee high enough to allow for a 10- or 12-hour work day.

- When assessing a project rate, lean toward the high side, which in essence builds an overtime bonus into your fee.

- Ask for a higher hourly rate than you would under ordinary circumstances.

If the client objects to your quote, that's when to explain that you are charging more than usual because this is a rush job. Repeat this term during negotiations as the client tries to talk down your fee. You'll get what you want if the client needs the job done yesterday.

- *You're expected to pay expenses out of your fee.* Some costs are inherent in all jobs, and consultants often absorb small expenses as part of the cost of doing business. But if you have to incur major expenses—not just courier fees but subcontractors' earnings—be sure to ask for enough to cover them, even if it means raising your price above the norm.

- *You have unique qualifications for a job.* A Ph.D. in aeronautical engineering who has worked for a large airplane manufacturer and has a pilot's license should feel justified in asking for more than less qualified contractors when consulting about airline safety.

- *You are setting up a template or a pattern that your client will use in the future.* Start-up work can be time consuming, especially if it entails a lot of back-and-forth discussions and multiple submissions until the client is satisfied. A stingy client may then take the fruits of your labor and tell a less talented (and less expensive) free-lancer to follow the paradigm. Even if you are the contractor of choice for future work, you are not likely to put as much time into execution of the fifth of a series as you put into the premier. To ensure being adequately compensated for their creative work, consultants often charge extra when doing a template, a launch, or other substantial initial work.

- *The going rate is much too low for the work involved.* Sometimes what the market will bear simply is not enough. One of my sideline ventures, of which I am particularly proud because of its uniqueness, is creating crossword puzzles. If I accepted the standard payment offered by the major crossword publishers, I would earn about two cents an hour. I therefore decided to create puzzles only for corporate clients who are willing to pay much more than the going rate. Because my fee is high, I do not have much crossword business. But I feel justified pricing the puzzles according to what they are worth, not what the general market expects to pay. Not everyone can do this work, so those who can should be amply rewarded.

- *You really don't want a particular job, but you expect to be paid handsomely if you do get it.* A job can lack appeal for many reasons: it may be uninteresting, the client may be difficult, or it may come at a bad time. If your gut tells you to turn down the work but your head says to pursue it, price it high. Whenever you regret taking on the assignment, you'll be able to console yourself with the thought of a hefty paycheck.

## Below the Bottom

In the ideal world, independent contractors would land far more high-paying jobs than low-paying ones. In reality, the reverse tends to be true. Consultants often find themselves accepting work at the bottom of the pay scale—or even lower.

In general it's a mistake to take work that pays peanuts. The time you invest on that job could be better spent prospecting for better-paying work, cleaning your files, learning new software, or doing other tasks of business management. Although I would never urge a freelancer to take a job that pays less than the norm, I can conceive of several situations in which working for a pittance is acceptable. I have offered my services at low cost or next to nothing in each of these circumstances:

- *You are dealing with a new client with whom you would like to establish a relationship.* Accepting a low fee under these circumstances could backfire unless you clearly spell out the situation in advance. Be sure the client knows that this is an introductory fee and that you expect to charge more in the future. Also, do not take on a big project for a low fee. Agree to work at a low, introductory price only for a small job.

- *You _really_ want a job, but you know the client can't afford the going rate.* Sometimes a job has a lot of appeal but the client does not have a lot of money. If you really want the job and are willing to accept less pay than usual, go ahead and take it. But be sure the client knows that you are undercharging; you don't want this low fee to set a precedent if you are referred for other work. Also, as part of the fee, ask for some sort of nonmonetary compensation, such as a package of services or products that the client produces or referrals to more lucrative business.

- *You believe in a cause and are willing to offer your professional services pro bono or at reduced cost.* We are more than independent businesspeople; we also are individuals who care about particular issues. Sometimes we choose to give our professional services to our favorite charity or cause at little or no charge. The operative word here is *choose.*

André is a professional fund-raiser who has a pet cause, literally: animal rescue. He has personally adopted or found homes for seventeen stray cats. When he heard that an animal rescue organization was trying to increase its revenue, André volunteered to mastermind their campaign. He offered to do this time-consuming task without payment, but on two conditions: his work would be acknowledged in the organization's newsletter, and he would receive a pair of tickets to the group's $500-a-plate dinner. At the dinner, André made contact with several people who were interested in hiring him as a consultant for their own fund-raising programs. He received calls from several other people who read about him in the newsletter. In the end, André figured he snared at least four new clients by doing pro bono work for a cause he supported.

So when is it acceptable to work for less than the going rate? When you have decided to do so, not when you have been backed into a corner by a client who refuses to pay an acceptable fee. Under no circumstances should you agree to work for less than the market will bear only because the client is too cheap to come up to market standards.

When I am approached by a skinflint who will not pay a reasonable rate, I turn down the job. Then the client will often ask, "Could you recommend someone else?" I reply, "I know many freelancers, but I don't know anyone who is willing to work for that little." Unfortunately, that is not true; when desperate for work, some freelancers will accept any job, no matter how low the pay. That is why the bottom of the going-rate range is so much lower than the top.

By turning down ridiculously low rates, we won't necessarily make the spread of the going rate more narrow. If the top of the range is very high, as we hope it is, the bottom will seem quite low. But if we refuse to work at an unreasonable rate, all of our colleagues will reap the benefits. The market will bear more, and the term *struggling freelancer* will disappear from our language.

# 5

# What Comes After "Hello"?

AFTER BEING self-employed for only about a month or so, I attended my first meeting of the Editorial Freelancers Association. The speaker that evening (whose name unfortunately escapes me) gave what was probably the most important advice I have ever heard in my career as an independent businesswoman.

That advice was simple: Do not let a client pressure you into a price commitment when you first discuss a job. Offer to call back with a price. If the client insists on knowing your fee that day, call back in a few hours. In the interim, consider what you know about the assignment. Think about everything the client mentioned. Weigh the unspoken ramifications. Then come up with a fee for what you perceive the job really is.

I had a chance to put this advice into action the day after I heard it. A client called to ask if I could take on a new job. As she described it, I made mental notes about what I thought it was worth. Then she asked the inevitable: "How much will you charge?"

I was about to quote a figure that was bouncing around in my head when I remembered the advice of the night before. "I'll have to get back to you with a price," I said.

43

I then took pad and pen and expanded on the notes I had made during the discussion with the client. In addition to what she had indicated the job would entail, I noted other tasks that could crop up in the course of the assignment, work the client had not specifically mentioned but that was a logical aspect of the job. Being very new to freelancing, I didn't have many log sheets; and those I did have were not as detailed as the ones I now keep. I knew instinctively, however, that my fee should be based on how long I thought the job, as I now envisioned it, would take. If my time estimate was accurate, my first guess at the fee was much too low. But I wasn't even sure if the fee I now had in mind was reasonable. So I called two friends who did similar work and asked their opinions. When my colleagues learned that the client was an advertising agency, both replied that I should charge much more than I was considering. Ad agencies, they reminded me, are the plushest segment of our industry and expect to pay top dollar.

When I called the client back with a price, it was almost three times as high as the figure that had come to mind when we had initially talked. I held my breath, fearing I would lose the job because my fee was too steep. Much to my relief, the client said, "That's a bit high, but if you think that is what it will take, I guess we'll have to go with it. Can we call your figure a cap? If you can bring it down on your final invoice, I'd appreciate it."

Had I responded with my gut reaction when the client first asked for my fee, I would have grossly underpriced this job. Time and again, this experience has been repeated. I know that I tend to be a lowballer, so I coach myself to make my first guesstimate higher than my gut reaction. Even so, it is almost always lower than the bid I eventually present. If I bend too soon to a client's urging for a quote, I almost always regret the words that come from my lips.

## The First Rule of Pricing

Not coming up with a price when initially asked is what I call the first rule of pricing for the consultant. For my money, there is only one other rule of pricing, which is introduced in Chapter 8, "Know Your

Bottom Line." If you consistently apply these two rules, you are practically guaranteed an income that will please you.

Now here is the first half of the strategy that will make you content with your pricing decisions:

> *Rule No. 1. Never quote a price on the spot. First get as much information as you can about a job. Then take time to assess the project thoroughly and calculate the best rate.*

This rule actually has three parts:

1. Don't quote a price when first asked.

2. Learn everything you can about the job.

3. With this information, and considering other facts or impressions about the client, similar jobs you've done in the past, your workload, the job's schedule, and other factors that can affect your price, determine what you want to charge.

Failure to heed any part of Rule No. 1 can stick you with a price you wish you could change. In the story opening this chapter, if I had stated my fee when first asked, it would have resulted in a price that was far too low for a client with a generous budget.

Brian, a public relations consultant, had an unfortunate experience because he failed to learn everything about a job. He had run a successful business for several years and knew what he could command for producing a twelve-page, full-color brochure. Even so, he obeyed the first part of Rule No. 1, waiting a day before calling the client to quote his customary charge. During this call, Brian should have generated more discussion about the assignment. He assumed that his fee would cover only the creative work, because all his other clients routinely footed the bill for production. This client, however, assumed that Brian's fee included the cost of printing the 10,000 brochures. The client refused to pick up even a portion of the printer's bill, which ate up most of Brian's fee.

Nancy is in the rapidly growing field of medical billing. When she first met with a five-physician orthopedic practice, she did not discuss her fee. She gathered as much information as she could during that visit, then called a few days later with follow-up questions. However, when setting her fee she failed to consider everything the client had said. The physicians had told her that almost half of their patients were employees of a large construction company, which self-insured its workers. The practice also handled orthopedic care for three smaller companies that managed their employees' health coverage, instead of dealing with an insurance company or managed care plan. Knowing that every insurance company has its own forms and procedures, Nancy should have realized that she would have to learn their systems when dealing with these four self-insured companies. When she calculated her fee, she did not allow extra time for this learning curve or for billing companies whose primary business was not insurance. Nancy did well for this client when handling bills for the insurance companies and managed care organizations she knew from her other customers. However, her hourly rate equivalent was substantially less when processing bills for the self-insured companies. The large one had complicated record-keeping systems that necessitated printing out bills in triplicate—which tied up Nancy's printer for hours. Because she didn't do much billing for the smaller self-insurers, each time she did so she felt almost as if she was starting from scratch to learn their procedures.

These cases illustrate how failure to apply any part of Rule No. 1 can lead to poor pricing decisions. Take time to contemplate the price you will need to charge for a job. Don't let your fee be one of the first things you discuss.

## What to Do Between the Question and the Answer

As Rule No. 1 states, before you name your price you are going to get all the information you can about the job and do thorough calculations. This simple statement translates into a number of activities. Most of them will be familiar because they were discussed in earlier chapters. A few other points will be described in more detail in the following chapters.

- Start a list of questions you neglected to ask or points the client failed to mention. As you continue with the following steps, add to this list. Do not call every time you have a question, unless you want the client to become annoyed with you before you have even begun the job. Save the questions until you have completed the following steps.

- List the tasks the client told you were part of the job. Expand the list with other tasks that you assume must be done to complete the assignment.

- Check your log sheets from other projects that involved these tasks. Note how long it took you to do each task. If possible, look up information from several projects, not just one.

- Talk to other consultants to find out the going rate for this type of work and this type of client.

- Consider different pricing methods. Do you want to charge by the hour? Propose a flat fee for the project? Ask for a per diem rate? Use some other method or combination of methods?

- Determine the fee you would like to charge. Then decide how low you're willing to go if the client won't pay this much. Think of what you would like as compensation if you agree to do the job for less than your top offer. You'll learn more about this in Chapter 8.

## Don't Be Afraid to Ask

When you have completed these steps, you may have listed quite a few questions. This is the time to make the follow-up call. Be sure that the client understands that you are not quite ready to quote a price; you simply are calling for further clarification. Do not be pressured into stating your fee until you have answers to all your questions and you have considered how any new information will affect your price.

## What should you do about a slow-paying client?

First, how do you define slow paying? Some consultants complain about clients who take more than two weeks to pay. I am satisfied with a client who pays within four to six weeks.

An entire book could be written on the subject of slow-paying clients. But because this book is about pricing strategies, let's confine this discussion to a few suggestions on billing techniques when working for check-writers who move at a snail's pace:

- *Ask for staggered payments.* For a slow payer, send the first invoice when you return the signed contract, before you actually begin work on the project. With luck, you will see at least some of the money by the time the job is finished or shortly thereafter.

- *Charge more than you ordinarily would.* The extra fee could easily be eaten up with the time you spend making follow-up calls to the accounts payable department and writing dunning letters. A slow-pay "bonus" will compensate for your negative cash flow.

The specific questions you ask will, of course, vary with the type of work you do and what you already know—and don't know—about the assignment. Regardless of your specialty, however, certain points should be raised in either your first or second contact. The answers could affect your pricing decision.

- *What is the client expecting to pay?* This question is one way to determine what the market will bear. Chapter 4

- *Use an incentive system.* Determine the fee you want, and make that your bottom line. Go no lower, but do go higher—if the payment is late. In your contract, indicate the fee you have agreed to, and also state that if you have not been paid by a particular date, a surcharge of, say, 10 percent will be added. Include the same language on your invoice to remind the client that prompt payment will save the company money.

- *Do not accept more work from a client who owes you a bundle.* When a delinquent client calls with another assignment, reply, "I would like to do it, but I can't until you pay me for the last job." I tell my slow payers that I have a policy of not accepting more work from a client who owes me more than a certain amount. (This value depends on how much the client is in arrears.) I add that I will be glad to discuss the assignment as soon as I receive a check that brings the client's debt below this amount. Some clients go off in a huff and find a more "amenable"—translation: gullible—consultant. I don't care that I've lost the business. This is the type of client I am happier without.

described how to probe for what the client thinks is a reasonable fee.

- *When is the project due?* If you have to work on a tight deadline, you might want to charge a rush fee.

- *Who will handle expenses?* Consultants expect to cover some expenses as part of the cost of doing business. But you shouldn't be expected to foot huge bills. If a job will incur major expenses, such as the hiring of subcontractors, substantial long-distance or international phone calling and faxing, or production costs, you should clarify who will pay for them.You don't want to find yourself in a position like the public relations consultant, Brian, who had to pay for printing brochures that he assumed his client was covering. Be as specific as possible. Don't just ask the client who will cover expenses. Instead, say something like, "Do you want me to pay the subcontractors from my fee?" Or, "I'll pay for phone calls, but I expect you to handle the logistics and costs of shipping."

- *How many times will you be seeing the job?* Consultants may normally expect to revise their work after the client has looked over their submission and made suggestions. But a revision does not entail going back to square one. You shouldn't have to do a job over entirely if a client has given you bad directions, changed his or her mind, or reconceived the project. Nor should you have to go over and over and over your work until a picky client is 100 percent satisfied. Find out how many revisions the client expects you to make, and price the job accordingly. When you submit your bid, indicate how many revisions the fee covers. Be sure the client understands that any additional reviews will be billed on a separate schedule.

- *Can you do interim billing?* Most clients accept interim bills on big projects. Common variations are monthly bills on long-term projects and payments in thirds on large-budget jobs (one-third at the beginning, one-third at the midpoint, and one-third upon submission of the finished product). Of course, you can submit bills as often as you want; it's how swiftly they are paid that counts. Which brings us to the next question.

- *How quickly does the client pay?* A slow-paying client in effect is holding money owed you and collecting interest you could be earning. Some consultants charge more if they know that the client is slow paying. What if you don't expect collection problems? You cannot bill for the time you spend on the phone with the accounting department or writing dunning letters. If you have any reason to believe that you may have to play bill collector, make your fee high enough to allow for these wasted hours.

You may be able to cover all these issues in your initial conversation. Even so, save a question or two for a follow-up call, especially if you have never worked with a particular client. You can learn a lot from the way the client responds to your questions. Also, as the client answers your queries, both you and the person you will be working with may think of other relevant points.

When Carlos, a consulting engineer, called to go over some details before making his bid, he discovered that the client had forgotten about a previous engineer's report. "It completely slipped my mind, and besides it's two years old," the client apologized. He was reluctant to part with the entire report but did agree to fax Carlos the summary. In reviewing it, Carlos realized that he had to examine several more areas of the structure he was being hired to assess, and accordingly increased his fee to cover these previously unknown tasks. He interpreted the faxing of the summary as a sign that the client would be amenable if the project ran into snags that required a cooperative effort. Had the client refused to share this information, Carlos might have raised his fee in anticipation that this company or individual could be difficult to work with.

## Red Flags

As Carlos discovered, a client may reveal important information in a follow-up conversation that he or she forget to mention when you first talked. Sometimes it's not what the client says but how he or she responds that gives you the most insight into what working for this customer would be like. Carlos believed that his client was being honest when he said he forgot about the previous engineer's report, and his willingness to share the highlights of the report suggested that this would be someone good to work with.

Various warning signs may indicate that a client might not be a good partner. If you detect any of the following red flags, you probably will want to price the job on the high side to cover the added time and frustration of dealing with a difficult client or an uncertain situation.

- *The client does not return your phone calls.* Be sure your fee is not dependent on meeting deadlines if you think your client is telephone shy. The client's unavailability by phone could sabotage your schedule—not just on this job but on others that you are working on simultaneously.

- *The contact dithers when responding to your questions.* The client could be someone who is disorganized, does not do well unless in control, or buckles easily in stressful situations. If these personality traits can affect your work, be sure you ask for enough money in compensation.

- *Nobody seems to accept ownership of the job.* Smell trouble when the person in charge or a subordinate shows little interest in the job. You may have trouble getting all the important information that can affect your price, the time you'll need, or the scope of the project. Also, a reluctant employee is not likely to be much help if you have difficulty collecting your payment.

- *The job changes substantially during initial discussions.* If the job grows every time you talk to the client, or if it changes direction entirely, you could be in big trouble. A client who can't foresee what the job entails and what the finished product should look like, or who can't communicate this vision to the freelancer, is likely to be displeased with the work no matter how well it is executed. You may have to do it over to please this wishy-washy client. Don't agree to a flat fee if the client cannot define the job and stick to this description.

- *The client admits that the pay is low but offers you steady work.* Don't be trapped into a major commitment for such a client. Make this client only a small part of your workload so you have time for higher-paying jobs.

- *The job requires you to work on the client's premises five days a week.* This schedule will leave you no time to pursue work with other clients. A short-term job of this nature might be fine, but a long-term arrangement could ruin your consulting business. Besides, are you really an independent contractor when you show up at someone else's office every day for months on end?

- *The client assures you that the job is small or easy.* Maybe it is a small fraction of the company's overall business. But the effort you may need to exert could be substantial. Don't assume that a job is simple just because the client says it is; evaluate it for yourself.

- *The client is vague about the payment schedule.* You can't pay your bills on the promise of money coming in; you need cash in hand. You might want to boost your fee to cover the time you could spend chasing down unpaid invoices. If a client owes you for past jobs, think twice before agreeing to do more work.

To sum up, you have a lot of homework to do before committing to a price. You need to evaluate both the specific project and the client in general. Your goal is to arrive at a fee that is fair for the time you will be devoting to the job and that reflects the realities of working with this particular client. This is especially important for work billed on a project basis, where you need to make a firm commitment for what is often a sizable chunk of time. If you price the job too low, you'll be penalized for the entire duration of the project. The next chapter therefore focuses exclusively on project rates and explains how to set fair—but pleasingly plump—flat fees.

# 6

# fair and fat flat fees

OF ALL the different methods of charging for freelance services, the one that presents the most difficulty is project pricing, or setting a flat fee for the job. If you commit to a project rate that turns out to be too low for the work involved and you haven't built in any safeguards that allow you to alter that fee, you will end up with a low hourly rate equivalent. You could, of course, inflate the bid, to be certain of making a decent rate should the project mushroom beyond expectations. But if you quote too high a price, the client may bypass you for another consultant who promises to do the work for less. The trick, then, is to come up with a flat fee that the client thinks is fair but that is also fat enough to ensure you adequate compensation for your time and effort.

Ideally, the project rate you arrive at will be more than adequate, resulting in an hourly rate equivalent that is much higher than what you could have earned if you had charged by the hour or by another method. Indeed, many consultants favor project pricing because they have found charging a carefully calculated flat fee to be the most lucrative pricing method. This has certainly been my experience. In addition, as later chapters point out, a high hourly rate equivalent on project-rate jobs can enhance your attitude about the value of your services, leading you to raise your fees.

Many of the strategies discussed in earlier chapters are aimed at making project rates successful. For openers, you'll want to learn the going rate—both what other consultants are currently earning for this type of work and what the client considers acceptable. You'll need to put together as much information as possible about the job. You will probably try several different methods to calculate the fee. For example, you might estimate how many days the job should take and multiply that number by your per diem rate. You should also consider what specific tasks are involved and work out how long it will likely take to do each.

## Translating Traders' Talk

Let's look at how Jean, a consultant to the financial services industry, approached setting a project fee for one of her clients, a large mutual fund company. To attract more small investors who were not well versed in the language of Wall Street, the company wanted to recast a prospectus for a mutual fund into consumer-friendly terms. The job had to be completed within a month. The client asked Jean, as well as several other consultants, to bid on the project on a flat-fee basis.

Although she had worked for this client before, Jean had never done an assignment like this. Her first step in setting a fee, therefore, was to attempt to learn the going rate. She knew this client generally was willing to pay top dollar, so she felt confident that she could ask a lot—once she figured out the typical range for this type of work. Accordingly, she called some acquaintances who also did consulting work for the financial services industry to check with them about appropriate fees. Predictably, their suggestions varied, but one consultant came up with a method that Jean had not considered: charging by the page.

Jean assumed that she would not be able to take on any other big assignments during the month she was working on this "translation" project. Small, ongoing jobs with her regular clients would occupy any free working hours. Jean subtracted from her monthly income goal the earnings from those ongoing jobs with other clients. The difference was the minimum that this assignment would have to bring in to meet her financial target.

After toying with the page-rate approach, Jean considered the number of days available to work on this project, given the rest of her workload and other commitments. Then she multiplied that number by her per diem rate. Finally, Jean focused on the tasks involved in the assignment. She listed all the activities that she could think of, consulted her log sheets from past projects to estimate how long each task would take, totaled the estimated hours, and multiplied that figure by her hourly rate goal.

By the time she had gone through this process, Jean had several rates to choose from. These rates were based on:

- The pay scale of the client
- Other consultants' earnings for similar work
- Jean's monthly income goal
- A page rate
- A per diem rate
- The total number of hours estimated for completing each task

Analyzing the results of these different pricing strategies, Jean decided to ask $5,600 for the project. This fee was not at the very top of the range of the various pricing methods, but it was also far from the lowest figure she had calculated. Jean did not want to offer too low a bid, which could short-change her if she had misjudged the work involved. Her fee seemed appropriate for a time-consuming job from a client with deep pockets.

As it turned out, Jean did not get the job—but not because of her price. Five people submitted bids. Three of them, including Jean's, were about $5,500. The lowest bid was $3,500; the highest was twice Jean's price. The contract was awarded to one of the three consultants who wanted about $5,500. Jean thinks he got the job because he had done similar work for this client before—not because his price was better.

## Putting Your Project Logs to Use

The most laborious method that Jean used to calculate her project rate was the last one: estimating how long it would take to complete all the tasks. Although working out this estimate can be time consuming, many consultants—myself included—have found that it is the method with the best, and most useful, results. For starters, it makes you consider what you know about the job and leads you to recognize what else you need to find out. With the task-based approach, your fee is predicated on your own working style and experience. If you are slow at certain tasks but you base your project rate on your personal working speed, the fee will be fair for the hours you need. Finally, if you augment your charge to allow for the unforeseen but nothing untoward occurs, you will earn much more than you had anticipated when you set your rate.

The key to task-based project rates will be found in your own files: the logs you have kept for past projects. From these logs you will be able to estimate how long it might take you to do the job you are pricing. Chapter 3 explained how to prepare these logs while you were working on an assignment. Now you will learn how to use the logs to price new projects.

Setting a project rate according to the tasks involved entails a series of seven steps. These are outlined below and in the worksheet template in Figure 3.

1.  List all the tasks you think you will have to perform for the job.

2.  Go through your logs from past projects to see how long it took you to do similar tasks for other assignments. (This process will not be difficult if your project logs are easily accessible. I keep mine in the front of each project folder. Other consultants may prefer to use a computerized database.) You might need to check several project logs to obtain time estimates for all the tasks involved in the new project. If the project includes tasks you have never done before, take a stab at how long you'll need for them.

### Figure 3
### Template for Calculating a Task-Based Project Rate

Task 1          _____ hours
Task 2          _____
Task 3          _____
Task 4          _____
Task 5          _____

**Total Hours** _____

**Hourly Rate** $_____

**Total Hours × Hourly Rate = $**_____

**Expenses**                              $_____

**Other Factors** _____

_____

**Final Bid**                             $_____

3. Once you have estimated the time needed for each task, tally the hours.

4. Multiply the total hours by the hourly rate you would like to earn.

5. Add enough money to cover expenses you will be expected to handle.

6. Adjust the rate. For example, you could increase the fee to protect yourself against unforeseen hitches that might add to your time on the job. You might also modify the fee to account for factors that cannot easily

be translated into numbers. For instance, you might raise the fee if you anticipate losing weekends to meet a tight deadline for a difficult client. On the other hand, you could decide to eat some costs when working for a nonprofit organization with a limited budget but extensive referral possibilities for lucrative work later.

7.  Determine your final bid.

## The More Numbers, the Better

Some project pricers end the process here. In my experience, however, the most successful project pricing results from using far more numbers. I prefer to calculate three time-estimate scenarios and multiply the total hours by two, three, or maybe even four hourly rates.

When you use a single time estimate for each task, you'll be aiming for an average figure. But what if the job is more complicated than average? Then you'll put in more hours than anticipated and won't be fairly compensated for all your time. If you've never done a given task, your guesstimate of how long it will take may be way off base, warping the accuracy of your total time estimate.

I therefore like to assume three scenarios when I estimate the time for each task:

- *Everything goes exceptionally smoothly.* This scenario indicates the fewest hours the job will take. This yield is the lowest fair price.

- *The job is fairly typical—although it has no unexpected snags, it takes a while to do.* This scenario indicates the average number of hours you can anticipate for the job and is probably similar to the single-scenario estimate already described. The price you estimate using these numbers will be in the middle range: fair but neither fat nor scant.

- *Every task is more complicated than usual.* This scenario assumes that nothing goes well. The job is fraught with every calamity imaginable—plus other disasters you never could have foreseen. The bottom line will be the highest price you could dare to ask and the most you would be able to earn if you were being compensated on an hourly basis. The fee may seem fat, but it would be fair if you had to log an extraordinary amount of time.

When you apply this triple-scenario strategy to estimate a project rate, you can use more information from your past experience. If you have done many jobs that involved the same task, you'll have data for the low, average, and high scenarios. But should your project logs mention a specific task only once or twice, you won't have to assume that your limited experience was typical; you can guess at best-case and worst-case possibilities also. If you've never done a task before, you'll want a broad range for your time guesstimate.

In addition to using three estimates of the time needed to complete each task, you could multiply the total hours by more than one hourly rate. The extra calculations take practically no time. You simply multiply three numbers—the fewest hours you would need for a cream-puff job, the average, and the most time you would log for a job from hell—by several hourly rates. You might use the following fees:

- The rate you expect to earn
- A higher rate you aspire to
- A lower rate you are willing to work for if you cannot earn as much as you would like
- The lowest acceptable rate for this type of client
- The rate your highest-priced competitor charges

When you have completed these calculations, you'll have a lot of numbers. Now what do you do with this confounding array of fees?

## Zeroing in on a Fair and Fat Fee

The best way to understand how to manage this number overload and to recognize the advantages of this complex pricing strategy is to work through an example. In this hypothetical case the type of work done by the consultant, whom we'll call Fred, is irrelevant. His tasks are identified only by number. This lack of detail will help you concentrate on how Fred manages the information at his disposal.

The worksheet for Fred's triple-scenario, multiple-rate, task-based estimate is shown in Figure 4. The column titled "Least" represents the fewest hours the job could take, resulting in the lowest charge for any given hourly rate. The "Average" column is probably similar to what Fred would estimate if he used a single scenario. The "Most" column anticipates the greatest number of hours each task could take and reveals the highest fair rates if the job turns out to be a monster.

In each of these scenarios, Task 3 takes the most time. This is the work that the client probably uses to describe the job. The help-seeking client would tell a software developer, for instance, "We need a program to...." Note that Task 3 represents only 33 percent to 40 percent of the total hours estimated for the job. Even when Task 3 is combined with the second most time-consuming activity (Task 4), less than two-thirds of the total estimated hours are accounted for. This demonstrates an advantage of the task-based approach to project pricing. If Fred had based his flat fee on only how long he might take to complete the one or two most obvious activities, he would have grossly underestimated the time commitment for the job and probably would not have charged enough. The task-based approach makes the consultant think about everything the assignment entails and set a price accordingly.

The hour estimates that Fred used in each of these scenarios were based on data in his logs for past projects, with a few exceptions. He had performed Task 5 only twice before. The first time it took five hours; the second time, in a project that did not go very smoothly, it took six hours. Fred decided that this task would always require about the same amount of time, so he made the spread over the three scenarios rather narrow. On the other hand, he made the time-estimate range broader for Task 6, a chore with which he had no experience.

### Figure 4
### Triple-Scenario, Multiple-Rate
### Task-Based Estimate Worksheet

|  | Least | Average | Most |
|---|---|---|---|
| **Task** | **Estimated Hours Required** | | |
| Task 1 | 5 | 7 | 10 |
| Task 2 | 3 | 4 | 5 |
| Task 3 | 12 | 20 | 35 |
| Task 4 | 8 | 14 | 20 |
| Task 5 | 4 | 5 | 6 |
| Task 6 | 4 | 7 | 10 |
| **Total Hours** | 36 | 57 | 86 |

**Hourly Rate × Hours Above**

| | | | |
|---|---|---|---|
| #1—$50 | $1,800 | $2,850 | $4,300 |
| #2—$70 | $2,520 | $3,990 | $6,020 |
| #3—$85 | $3,060 | $4,845 | $7,310 |

| **Expenses** | $100 | $150 | $300 |
|---|---|---|---|

**Other Factors:** Client generally tight with money.

**Final Rate** (above rate plus expenses)

| | | | |
|---|---|---|---|
| #1 | $1,900 | $3,000 | $4,600 |
| #2 | $2,620 | $4,140 | $6,320 |
| #3 | $3,160 | $4,995 | $7,610 |

When the hours estimated for each of the three scenarios were totaled, the difference was substantial. If everything went perfectly smoothly, the job could be completed in about 36 hours. More likely, it would take around 57 hours. However, if the project turned into a nightmare, Fred could expect to log about 86 hours. With this multiple-scenario method of setting project fees, it is not at all unusual for the highest hour estimate to be two or three times greater than the lowest. That does not mean the estimates were faulty; the disparity merely reflects the fact that consulting work is not always predictable. This pricing strategy steers the bidder toward prices that offer adequate rewards despite the vagaries of the consulting business.

Fred multiplied his three hour tallies by three rates. He hoped to earn $70 an hour; if he had been setting a price based on a single rate, it would in fact have been $70. However, he knew this client ran a tight ship and rarely paid more than $50 when contracting out work on an hourly rate basis. Because Fred had earned $85 an hour from more generous clients, he used this figure as his high-rate goal.

The out-of-pocket costs on this job would not be great—mostly long-distance calls and faxes and postage. Fred doubted that he'd actually shell out $150 on expenses, but to be safe he made this his middle-of-the-range figure. And he doubled it for the highest estimate, in case the extra time to complete each task entailed a lot more telephoning and mailing.

To arrive at his final figures, Fred added the expenses for each scenario to the project fees based on the three hourly rates. This gave him a dizzying array of nine numbers, ranging from $1,900 to $7,610.

Does this gigantic spread impress you as an exercise in futility? It's not. These numbers reveal a lot of useful information:

- If everything went perfectly smoothly, the least Fred could expect from a client with a tight budget would be $1,900. Of course, rarely does a job go perfectly smoothly. Furthermore, the whole point of working for a flat fee is to take home more than is possible when working for a tightwad who pays by the hour. Therefore, no consultant would want to charge anything near the lowest of the nine numbers derived with this method.

- If the job turned out to be a disaster and Fred still wanted to earn top dollar, he'd have to charge $7,600. He knows that the client is not generous, however, and is unlikely to pay this much. In general, the highest number calculated in this nine-fee scenario is higher than any client would consider reasonable, because it represents a good deal for a consultant in a project gone bad—not a situation clients want to contemplate.

- Suppose for a minute that Fred really doesn't want this job. Maybe the work is coming at a bad time, or perhaps he doesn't like the client. In that case, he would lean toward the high end. If he were to bid $7,000 to $7,500, the client would probably choose a different consultant. But should Fred get the job at that rate, he could remind himself as he sweated through it that he was making a bundle for the hassle.

- Even if the job became a disaster, Fred would still make as much as he hoped ($70 an hour) if he charged $6,300.

- Fred suspects that this penny-pinching client would scream at anything over $4,500. At that rate, he'd make more than $70 an hour if the job turned out to be an average assignment. He'd come close to the minimum acceptable rate of $50 an hour if all hell broke loose and he needed to work about 85 hours. This hourly rate equivalent might not make Fred happy, but it could be the most the client would accept whether he charged by the hour or by the project.

- Suppose the client insisted on paying no more than $4,000. This figure is much more than Fred would earn for a snag-free job at the highest rate he has considered. It's slightly less, though, than he hoped to make for a typical job. But if Fred overestimated the time for one or two tasks in the "Average" scenario and he had almost no expenses, he'd be right on target. The same could be said if his estimates were too high for the "Most" scenario and he was content with a little more than $50 an hour.

   Based on this analysis, Fred decided to ask for $4,500. This figure would allow him to make his desired rate ($70 an hour) if the project went a little worse than he anticipated in his "Average" scenario. If it went really badly, he'd still earn more than $50 an hour provided his expenses were low.

   Fred felt a little anxious when he set this fee, uncertain how accurately he had guessed the time for each task. He needn't have worried. When using many numbers to estimate a job, plenty of opportunities arise for mistakes to balance out. Some task-time guesses will hit the nail on the head, but some may be too high, others too low. With any luck, at least one task will go much faster than anticipated and the extra time will compensate for underestimates on other tasks.

   Let's assume that Fred's client accepted his project rate of $4,500. Suppose that Fred logged 59 hours on this project (slightly more than the "Average" estimate) and had only $80 in out-of-pocket costs (less than his "Least" estimate). His hourly rate equivalent therefore would be ($4,500 – $80) ÷ 59 = $74.92. This is greater than the $70 an hour he was originally aiming for. Because Fred is a fictional consultant, let's alternatively assume a worst-case scenario. If he worked 75 hours and had costs of $180, his hourly rate equivalent would be $57.60. Either way, Fred would earn more than he could have if he had charged by the hour. Remember, he thought this client was likely to draw the line around $50 an hour, but he could make more than that by assessing a carefully calculated project fee.

## To Everyone's Advantage

The main reason to work for a flat fee is to earn more than you could if you charged by the hour. For this reason, I call flat fees "fat." But they are also fair, because you are being appropriately compensated for the amount of time and effort involved. Clients also feel that flat fees are fair; they won't agree to a project rate that drives them over budget. They don't care how long a consultant spends on a job, provided the work is done well, on time, and within budget.

Your exercises in arriving at project rates will represent time well spent. Your best bet is to try several methods to determine the fee. Then analyze all the information you have obtained and all the calculations you have made. With practice, you'll be able to shorten the bid-preparation time, and you'll go to the bank happy.

# 7

# Case Study: A Successful Project Rate

LIKE THE previous chapter, this one concentrates on project rates. Here we'll follow a freelancer as she discusses a job with a client, calculates the fee, and analyzes her pricing decision at the end of the job. Some steps in this process will be familiar because they were discussed in previous chapters. Other stages, such as negotiating, will be examined in more detail in following chapters. The entire process is presented here, at more or less the midpoint of the book, to show how all the pieces can come together to result in a successful pricing experience.

The freelancer in this case, Susan, is a writer. As I explain when I use this example in workshops for writers and editors, this freelancer is working not for the low-paying publishing industry but for a high-paying corporate client. The numbers in this case study may not seem high to consultants in professions more lucrative than writing. Whether the rates strike you as high or low, the *process* that Susan follows is the same no matter what the consultant's field. The strategies for setting project rates are similar for all independent professionals, although the actual dollars earned

will vary from one specialty to another—and also among the various clients of any self-employed individual.

## The Job Description

Eric, a public relations agent for a major food conglomerate, asked
Susan to write an issue of a newsletter. "People are so confused
about the latest dietary recommendations," he said. "We want to
put the matter into perspective. We already have a newsletter,
but this is beyond its usual scope. The newsletter is generally
written by staff and consists mostly of recipes and new-product
information. This issue will be more informative and won't include recipes. Its purpose is to educate the public and help people
decide what to eat to stay healthy."

Susan was immediately interested in the job. She'd been confused herself about what she'd been hearing lately: Should you give
up eating all animal products, or are vegans worse off than carni-
vores? If you don't drink regularly, should you start having a nightly
glass of wine? Are megadoses of vitamin C really a magic potion?
She asked Eric for more details about the assignment.

The publication, he said, would be sixteen printed pages,
but Susan needed to write only twelve pages' worth; ads and
corporate information would fill out the issue. Her assignment
was to do telephone interviews with five experts and turn each
interview into a 1,200-word article. She also had to write a brief
introduction. Eric had already contacted the experts, all of them
academic researchers. Susan made a note of this fact, which suggested that they might not be able to explain their research clearly
for the lay public. Then she heard the bad news. One of the
experts was French and another Japanese by birth (although she
had lived in the United States some twenty years). The Frenchman, who was the last person Eric contacted, said he would rather
write his own article than be interviewed. Eric then wondered if
perhaps some of the other experts might also prefer to do their
own writing. He told Susan that she would have to edit any submitted articles for consistency in tone and style with the pieces
she wrote. Also, she should provide suggestions for art to break

up the text. Eric hoped she could create a table for each article, to lend scientific flavor to the newsletter.

## A Smorgasbord of Pricing Strategies

At the end of their conversation, Eric asked Susan how much she wanted for this job. She responded, "What kind of budget do you have?"

Eric answered, "We usually do the writing ourselves, so there's no budget line for it. Keep this in mind when you give us an estimate."

After they said good-bye, Susan checked her project files for Eric's company and other clients. Previously, Eric had paid her $200 per double-spaced page (about 250 words) for various kinds of writing. Figuring that this assignment would be the equivalent of about 25 pages, Susan's first guess at a price was $5,000. When she had written newsletters for other clients, she had earned between $2,500 and $4,000. But they had been shorter, about half as many words as she needed to compose for this job. That meant she might be able to charge more, perhaps as much as $8,000.

To learn if that price seemed reasonable, Susan checked with friends who ran a public relations consulting business. They suggested prices ranging from $3,000 to $9,000.

Susan then tried a unit method of pricing, the basic unit being an article. For another client she had recently written several articles of similar length based on transcripts of meeting presentations. She had earned $850 for each article, which had seemed like a fair price. But this job was different in several ways. For one, the audience was the general public, rather than professionals who spoke the language of the experts, and she was going to have to boil down material for the average reader. Also, in most cases she had to conduct interviews and develop the articles from her notes. To account for these differences, she figured she should charge more than $850 per article. She thought that $1,200 per article was probably reasonable, which would bring her total project fee to $6,000. However, editing the articles that the experts wrote should go faster than writing from scratch. If she received material for editing in a format that her computer could accept, she could lower the rate to $600 per submitted article.

This possibility prompted Susan to begin a list of questions to ask Eric: Would the experts who wrote their own articles deliver them in a computer-compatible format? As she turned her attention to the specific tasks involved in the job, she became aware of other uncertainties. Did Eric need her interviews transcribed for the company's files? If so, would he handle the arrangements, or did he expect her to do the typing herself or subcontract with a transcriber?

Realizing that her fee was greatly dependent on the transcription issue and the number of articles she would edit rather than write, Susan decided to call Eric. He told her that transcripts were not necessary. When she asked how many experts he thought would want to do their own writing, Eric replied, "Maybe one other besides the Frenchman. Writing is torture, you know, for academics." He couldn't answer the question about computer compatibility. And he had new instructions: "Be sure to send the articles to the experts before you submit them to me. We want approved material ready to go to print."

Before hanging up, Susan again asked Eric about his budget. "I honestly don't know," he said. "I'm guessing around $4,000." Finally! With persistence, she had gotten the client to indicate what his market would bear. Unfortunately, it was much less than she was considering.

After this conversation, Susan altered the items on her task-based estimate worksheet. She removed the line coded with a question mark—"transcribe interviews"—and added two new tasks: "correspond with experts" and "input experts' changes." From the "costs" section of her worksheet she removed "transcriber" and added "postage." She planned to estimate costs for overnight and overseas postage, even though some reviewers might prefer fax or e-mail, because it is best to assume the more expensive transmission method.

Next, with her modified task list Susan scoured her files to determine how long she would probably need for all the aspects of this job. She used a triple-scenario estimate, taking a stab at the least, average, and most hours she should reasonably allow for the project. She worked with three hourly rate goals: $70 (the minimum she considered acceptable for this type of client), $85 (her usual rate when billing by the hour for this type of client), and $100 (her ultimate dream). Figure 5 (page 74) is her estimate worksheet.

## Zeroing in on the Bid

Susan's task-based estimate suggested that Eric's ballpark figure of $4,000 was fine if the job entailed an average amount of work but might be low if the project turned out to be on the complicated side. Any fee over $6,000 was probably unnecessarily generous. Susan might enjoy such high earnings, but Eric would doubtless balk at a fee some 50 percent more than he was anticipating. Charging $5,500 would enable Susan to make out very well, unless the job closely followed the worst-case scenario. If Eric insisted, she could come down to $5,000, a fee equivalent to her previously earned page rate of $200 for a 25-page manuscript. But suppose Eric thought that even $5,000 was too much. Could she do the job for less? Yes, she could go as low as $4,000 and still earn close to her ideal rate of $100 an hour if the project proved to be "average." But with so many unknowns, it was not wise to assume that this was going to be a typical job.

Furthermore, Susan was not about to concede easily. She felt that the project was worth at least $5,000, which is what she hoped to make at a minimum. If she had to bring down her price, she would lower it in stages. And she wanted something in return if Eric wouldn't meet her first offer, especially if she had to go under $5,000. Susan knew exactly what to ask for: samples of the printed newsletter. It was going to make a great handout to showcase her work for prospective clients.

Susan determined the stages in which she'd approach Eric with her bid:

- $5,500—her initial offer

- $5,000 plus 100 printed newsletters—her rejoinder if Eric refused her first bid

## Figure 5
## Triple-Scenario, Triple-Rate Estimate Worksheet for Calculating a Project Fee to Write a Newsletter

|  | Least | Average | Most |
|---|---|---|---|
| **Task** | **Estimated** | **Hours** | **Required** |
| Do interviews* | 2 | 3 | 6 |
| Review notes and/or tapes* | 1 | 3 | 7 |
| Write from notes/tapes* | 6 | 12 | 22 |
| Edit submitted articles* | 4 | 6 | 8 |
| Develop tables and art ideas | 2 | 4 | 8 |
| Write introduction | 1 | 2 | 3 |
| Correspond with experts | 2 | 4 | 6 |
| Make experts' changes | 1 | 3 | 6 |
| **Total Hours** | 19 | 37 | 66 |
| **Costs** | | | |
| Phone | $40 | $80 | $120 |
| Postage | $35 | $60 | $95 |
| **Total** | $75 | $140 | $215 |

**Hourly Rate × Total Hours + Costs**

| | | | |
|---|---|---|---|
| $70 | $1,405 | $2,730 | $4,835 |
| $85 | $1,690 | $3,285 | $5,825 |
| $100 | $1,975 | $3,840 | $6,815 |

**Other Factors:** Client expects to pay about $4,000; no budget line.

---

*Don't know how many articles will be written from interviews, how many submitted by experts for editing. Assume three interview-based articles for Least and Average scenarios, four for Most. Assume short interviews for Least scenario, long, complicated interviews and articles for Most scenario.

- $4,700, plus 250 printed newsletters—her final concession, she hoped

- $4,200, plus 250 printed newsletters, and no handling of experts' changes—if Eric wouldn't pay at least $4,700, he was going to have to do some of the work himself.

## One-on-One with the Client

With these terms of her offer clearly in mind, Susan called Eric to present her fee. "I'd like $5,500," she said.

A whistle escaped from Eric's lips. "That's a lot more than I was expecting. Can you do it for less?"

"Well, this isn't a cut-and-dried job. English isn't the first language of two of these experts."

"That's why we're hiring you. We know you can make them sound good. So how about it? Can you knock a thousand or so off the price?"

"I'll do it for $5,000—if you can throw in 100 copies of the finished product. It will be a good addition to my portfolio."

"Sure, that's no problem. I'll give you 200 copies if you like," Eric offered. "But your price is still a bit steep. How about $4,750?"

"That's only a difference in $250. Why don't we stay with $5,000? That's about $200 a page, which you've paid me before." Susan decided to hold firm to the figure that most pricing methods suggested as the bottom line. She was prepared to lose $250 in exchange for more newsletters, though, if Eric threatened to go elsewhere. This wasn't likely; his company had money to spare. Finally he relented.

Then they discussed the payment schedule. Susan asked for half the fee in advance. Eric suggested payment in thirds: $2,000 in advance, $1,500 when she sent drafts to the experts, and $1,500 when she completed the project.

"I'll be sending the experts drafts as I finish each one. It won't be all at once," Susan objected. "Can't I just bill you in halves? We're talking about a difference of only $500 between the first payments. That's just 10 percent of the total project fee."

"Okay," Eric conceded. "Bill us $2,500 now and the other $2,500 when you complete the job."

After they finished talking, Susan wrote Eric a letter of agreement summarizing their conversation. She described the assignment that she would complete and indicated a timetable for the job as well as the payment schedule. She stated that part of her compensation would be 200 copies of the newsletter. She included lines for both hers and Eric's signatures. Then she signed two copies of the letter and mailed them to Eric along with her first invoice and a note asking him to return one signed letter to her.

The entire process of fee setting, including discussion with the client, calculation of fees by various methods, and finalization of the agreement, proceeded over the course of a week and totaled five hours. Susan felt that it was time well spent. She understood the job better after looking at it in detail. The fee was appropriate for the work anticipated and for a client with deep pockets. Only time would tell if she had priced the job well.

## Doing the Job

Susan kept a detailed project log as she worked on this job; it appears as Figure 6. She ended up conducting four interviews and editing only the Frenchman's submission. The 47 hours Susan logged were considerably more than the 37 she had anticipated in the "average" scenario but far less than the estimate for the worst-case scenario. While her expenses were $20 more than expected in the "average" case, they were $55 less than the highest estimate.

Comparing her project log and her estimate worksheet, Susan saw that she had projected fairly accurately how much time she would need for each task. But the total time was higher than anticipated, because her project log included a few items that were not on her estimate worksheet. Before she began the interviews, she decided to do some background reading so she wouldn't sound ignorant when talking with the experts. Also, she met with the artist to discuss the design, something she had not anticipated. Actual project logs usually include tasks not listed on a task-based estimate worksheet—either because they were overlooked in the push to prepare a bid or because the job took on new

### Figure 6
### Final Project Log for Writing a Newsletter

| Task | Hours Required |
|------|:---:|
| Discuss with client | ½ |
| Background reading | 4½ |
| Interviews (4) | 3 |
| Review notes and tapes | 3 |
| Write articles from notes/tapes (4) | 14 |
| Edit submitted article (1) | 5 |
| Develop tables (3) | 3½ |
| Develop other art ideas | 2 |
| Write introduction | 1½ |
| Correspond with experts | 4 |
| Incorporate experts' changes | 2½ |
| Meet with artist, client | 2 |
| General administration | 1½ |
| **Total Hours** | 47 |

| Costs | |
|------|---|
| Phone | $85 |
| Postage | $75 |
| **Total Costs** | $160 |

angles as the work progressed. That's one reason to price above the average estimate when setting a project fee.

Susan's log sheet did not include the five hours she spent determining the bid. Because she could go through the pricing exercise but not land a job, Susan usually does not consider the fee-setting time to be part of the job; for her it is an uncompensated aspect of doing business. Other consultants incorporate the time spent arriving at a bid in the project log.

## End-of-Job Analysis

Susan worked on this newsletter off and on over the course of six weeks. By the time the job was done, she was anxious to clear it off her desk. Before she could file it away, though, she had one more task: to analyze her pricing decision.

Susan charged $5,000 for this project. From this gross income, she had to cover $160 in expenses. She worked a total of 47 hours. Therefore, her hourly rate equivalent for this project was $(5,000 - 160) \div 47 = \$102.98$.

Susan was extremely pleased when she saw the results of this calculation. Her earnings exceeded the $100 an hour she coveted and were far more than the $85 an hour she would have charged if billing on an hourly basis. Had she billed $85 an hour for 50 hours (47 hours worked plus 2 hours' equivalent in expenses, rounded up), she would have earned $4,250, or $750 less than her project fee.

In the past, Eric had paid Susan $200 a page, and she had chosen the project rate of $5,000 in part based on this page rate. But she had forgotten to count the introduction and tables, which brought the page count to thirty-two. At a project fee of $5,000, the thirty-two–page manuscript fell far short of the goal of $200 per page. Susan realized that she should be more careful in the future when using a page rate to determine a project fee.

Another method Susan had used in calculating her fee was to assume that writing an article from scratch was worth $1,200, editing a submitted article $600. She could not tell from her project log whether these prices accurately reflected the work involved. Although Susan's project log listed writing and editing separately, she did not know how to prorate the background reading, artwork, and dealing with the experts. In the future, she would make this breakdown if a project involved both editing and writing.

Overall, Susan was pleased with her pricing decision. She had set a project rate that allowed her to earn more than $100 for every hour worked, which was much more than she would have made if she had charged an hourly fee. She didn't buckle at her client's suggestion of a lower fee but instead negotiated a deal that was acceptable to both her client and herself.

Other freelancers, Susan knew from her conversations with colleagues, would have asked for more, perhaps even as much as $9,000. But they probably would have priced themselves out of the job. Although they might not have been content with $5,000, Susan saw that this fee, reflecting her own working pace and earnings goals, was satisfactory for her client and close to perfect for herself. This experience demonstrated to her that without any doubt her consulting services were worth $100 an hour.

# 8

# Know Your Bottom Line

CHAPTER 5 presented the first rule of pricing for independent contractors: Assess the job thoroughly before stating your fee. This chapter deals with the second rule of pricing. Like the first rule, this one warns the consultant to plan carefully before talking with a client. It also applies whether payment is by the hour, by the project, or by some other method. In essence, the second rule of pricing cautions the freelancer: Know your bottom line!

This caveat is more complicated than it first appears. Knowing your bottom line means that you must determine:

- What you want to charge

- The lowest amount you will accept

- Intermediate prices between what you want and the lowest acceptable amount

- Concessions you expect the client to make if you have to accept less than you want

When you determine your fee by using the methods we have discussed, you will zero in not only on your desired price but also on the lowest acceptable price for the job. If the difference between these two amounts is great, you probably won't want to drop to the lowest acceptable figure as soon as the client rejects your initial bid. Instead, you can bring your price down in stages. You can also ask for some kind of concession for agreeing to work for less than your initial offer.

The process being described here is, in a word, negotiating. Politicians and mediation professionals may thrive on negotiations, but most other people tend to shy away from the process. However disagreeable the prospect of negotiating may be to freelancers who are more interested in the creative aspects of their work than in its business facets, negotiating is an important part of self-employment. Skillful negotiating ensures that you will be properly rewarded for your talents and the services you provide.

The purpose of negotiating is simply to get the best deal for yourself. Eight times out of ten, this means persuading your client to part with the largest possible sum of money. Sometimes, though, you may find yourself negotiating nonmonetary issues related to how the job is done. Will you work in your own office or the client's? How much time will you be given to do the work? As a last resort, your negotiations may focus neither on payment nor on particulars about the job but on some sort of nonmonetary compensation that you feel is an appropriate expression of thanks for your services.

## Where to Start, When to Stop

Some consultants like to make their first offer higher than the fee they want. A client who doesn't blink considers this high fee reasonable, and the consultant fares better than anticipated. If the client objects to the price, the consultant still comes out well after backing off to the desired fee. Other consultants open with their actual price and negotiate, if necessary, to a lower acceptable amount.

Whether you start high or begin where you hope to end is a matter of personal preference and style. Although there's no right way, I urge caution in pricing above your goal with steady clients. After repeatedly talking down the price, they'll realize that your first quote is a bluff. Ultimately, your pricing plans may backfire if such clients continue to talk you lower and lower.

Where to start your bidding process is less important than where to stop: at your bottom line. If you must, negotiate to the lowest rate you consider acceptable, but go no lower. If you can't get the money you feel you merit, ask for something of value in exchange for a reduced fee. Under no circumstances should you allow a client to cajole you into accepting less than you have determined to be the value of the job and your special services.

This, in essence, is the second rule of pricing. This rule tells you to take the time necessary to determine your bottom line—the money you must make on the job and perhaps nonmonetary compensation—before you open negotiations with the client. Stick to that bottom line. Refuse to go lower, even if it means losing the job.

> *Rule No. 2. Before quoting a fee, determine the lowest acceptable rate—and the concessions to stipulate if you have to go that low. Never agree to work for less than you know a job is worth and your services merit.*

This is the second most important strategy for successful pricing. Buckling when a client rejects a fee has resulted in disappointment for many an independent contractor. Ask a consultant to describe a job that was disastrous from a financial perspective and you'll likely hear a tale about going against one's better judgment and accepting a price despite knowing that it was too low.

Many consultants diligently apply the first rule of pricing but then fail to apply the second one. Luis is typical. Rather than respond to a client's initial query about his fees, he took time to analyze the job and determine the best pricing strategy. After arriving at what he considered to be a fair price, he called the client and said he wanted $3,000. "That's much too high," the client objected. "Can you do it for $2,600?" Luis agreed, but later kicked himself for giving in so easily. He knew the job was worth at least $2,800 and realized he should have demanded that much at a minimum. If the client really couldn't afford the extra $200, he might have been able

# What's a good payment schedule for a long-term project or one paying a very high fee?

In certain circumstances, interim billing or staggered payment is highly desirable. You won't want to wait until a long-term project is completed to submit your entire bill. Also, rather than writing a single large check to a consultant, a client may prefer to draw down the company's resources more gradually.

The payment schedule is a matter you should discuss with the client during the negotiating phase of fee setting. Once you have agreed on a schedule, put it in writing. That is, be sure to include the payment schedule in your letter of agreement.

An interim billing schedule should aim for a pay-as-you-go plan, so that you are not owed for work you completed long ago. By the time the project is in its final stages, the client should owe you less than you have already been paid.

For a long-term project that you are pricing by the hour, day, retainer, or unit, you might establish a

to work out a deal that fit the client's budget while compensating him in some way for the shortfall.

## Creative Concessions

Negotiation is a process in which both parties must bend a little to come to acceptable terms. You may be able to negotiate strictly on financial terms. When Luis asked for $3,000 and the client countered with $2,600, the consultant could have said, "I need at least $2,800 for this assignment. Can we meet halfway?" Then, regular billing cycle, such as every two weeks. When working for a flat fee, divide your charge into parts. If you are earning $10,000 and you know the job will last five months, you could bill $2,000 each month. Writers are often paid in thirds: one third upon submission of the outline, another third with the first draft, and the final third after the revision. Modify this model to create a billing schedule that is relevant for the type of work you do.

What really counts is not how often you bill but how fast the client pays. Billing in stages gives you an upper hand should the client prove lax in processing invoices. After an appropriate interval (which will vary according to the client's usual or promised payment speed), remind the client that you are still waiting for a check. A second or third reminder notice might be more dramatic: Refuse to continue the work until you see the money that you have already earned. (Be careful with this tactic. Some clients do not take well to consultants who insist on being paid in a timely fashion, and you could risk losing a job in midstream or not being called for future work.)

if the client wouldn't budge, Luis might have suggested changing the job description, for example by sharing certain responsibilities with the client.

Another alternative is to suggest meaningful nonmonetary compensation as part of the payment. When I was starting out as a freelancer, I wanted one thing even more than good income: a byline. Articles bearing my name as author could help establish my credentials and bring in more work. If a client would not pay me what I asked, my response was likely to be, "I can do it for your price—if you give me a byline."

The exact negotiating points will vary according to the circumstances. Consider the following strategies, which are especially useful when charging a flat fee, if a client winces at your price and seems ready to show you the door:

- *Suggest sharing expenses with the client, or ask the company to pick up all costs.* This strategy is an excellent tactic if your fee is high because you are anticipating major costs. Let your client cover the expenses and pay you only for your labor.

- *Call your suggested project rate a cap, and say you'll try to make the final bill less.* This is a good solution if you think you might have overpriced a job. Keep a careful work log, and if you can afford to bill less, do so. Your client will appreciate it and likely reward you with more business. On the other hand, if you had accurately anticipated the effort you needed to expend, don't cheat yourself on your final bill. With luck your client won't gripe when you turn in work worthy of high compensation.

- *Agree to do most, but not all, of the job for the client's price.* Certain aspects of a job may not require a person of your expertise but could be handled by someone on your client's payroll. The client might prefer to keep the consulting budget tight and have in-house employees take on extra work. But be sure you concur on what part of the job you will leave for the client, and put it in writing (see Chapter 9).

- *Explain that you can do the job for less than you requested, but only if the deadline is extended.* Time is money, for both consultants and clients. If a client asks for a one-month commitment but is willing to pay for only three weeks of your time, you'll need to bring in other work to close that month's income gap. Commitment to another job means that you'll have less time available for the one under negotiation. To complete the work, your deadline will have to be extended. The logic of this argument may cause a client who needs a job done according to a firm timetable to reconsider your price.

Should a client refuse to pay what you feel your services are worth, you have every right to expect something in return for less money. In the case just cited, that something is more time. Think of other forms of nonmonetary compensation that are important to you—as the byline was vital to me. Use one of these moneyless awards as a bargaining tactic the next time a client bristles at your fee. This is an expecially effective ploy when a client has limited financial resources. Just be careful not to short-change yourself. In other words, ask for something that is as valuable to you as a check. You might consider one of the following "payments" you cannot deposit at the bank:

- Referral to potential clients that can afford to pay well or are prestigious names for your portfolio

- Products made by the client

- Products made by someone else that the client can obtain at a significant discount

- Something the client can get easily that would be hard for you to obtain

## Negotiations in Action

In one case a client with a tight budget needed to bring in a number of consultants. Each of the following candidates quoted fees that the client felt were too high, yet all of them got the work. These independent contractors prepared themselves before they began talking price with the client and went in knowing what the job was worth and what they wanted. The course of their negotiations took a different turn in each case.

Kerry caved in when the client said that her fee was too high. She agreed to lower it without receiving any concessions, even though she knew the job was worth more than she settled for. Kerry proved to be the only consultant hired by this company who was not content with her final take. She ended up swearing she would never work for this client again. (She should have vowed instead to improve her negotiating skills!)

Perry suggested splitting the difference between his bid and the client's counteroffer. Actually, he wasn't splitting the difference; he was reducing his fee to the next lowest rate he had determined to be acceptable for the job. The client thought Perry was quite reasonable, and he did such a good job that he subsequently was given another assignment at a higher rate.

Sari also offered to lower her rate, but the client said that the reduced fee was still too high. The client's counteroffer came in at less than Sari's bottom line. Refusing to go below the minimum acceptable rate for her unique skills, Sari was prepared to lose the job. She stuck to her guns, and the client wouldn't budge either. They broke off negotiations. Eventually the client, realizing that he wouldn't find a better consultant for less money, reapproached Sari. When asked for the lowest price that would bring her on board, Sari, who had already written off this job as history, took a chance and named a per diem rate above her bottom line. The client accepted the bid and later told Sari that he admired her for holding out for a fair fee.

Harry, who presented a project bid that he thought was more than ample, offered to make it a cap when the client objected to the fee. Then Gary presented a high project rate which the client admitted was acceptable as a maximum but asked him to try to come in for less. Harry was able to do the job much more quickly than anticipated and shaved 20 percent off his bill. Gary's part of the project was too time consuming to let him offer much of a discount. To make the client happy, though, he billed 2 percent less than his opening bid. Both independent contractors saw more work from this client in the future.

Negotiating costs turned out to be the saving grace for two other consultants, Mary and Barry. Mary said she could do her part for less if the client directly hired the help Mary had planned to engage as subcontractors. Agreeing, the client paid Mary a decent hourly rate for her work and brought in people at a lower rate to do the tasks she would have subcontracted. Upon learning that Barry's high project fee included substantial expenses, the client offered to absorb those costs in the company's overhead. Barry then resubmitted a bid that the client could afford.

Larry suggested that part of his assignment could be handled by the client's support staff. By redistributing various duties, the client was able to engage Larry's services at a price they both found reasonable. Similarly, Jerry felt that the final stages of his job could be handled by the company's employees. But he neglected to secure advance clearance from the client. Having logged what he considered to be enough hours for his fee, Jerry turned in his work, along with instructions for what yet needed to be done by the client's staff. Jerry was paid, but was never given another assignment by this client.

Finally, two other freelancers negotiated for noncash payment. Initially, Sherry said she could do the job for less than her asking price if she was given more time. The deadline, however, was set in stone, as was the price the client was willing to pay for her part of the project. Sherry wanted the work, so she offered a compromise: she'd do the job within the deadline at the client's stated fee, provided she received additional payment in kind—in this case china that the company produced, which cost several hundred dollars on the open market. Terry, a die-hard sports fan, also sought nonmonetary compensation as part of his fee. He knew that the client had season tickets to his favorite team's games. The team was hot, and tickets at the box office were scarce. When the client tried to talk down Terry's price, he agreed—provided he received four passes to upcoming games.

As these examples illustrate, there are many ways to successfully negotiate a price that the client can afford and that is appropriate compensation for the consultant. You simply need to know what you want, what you need, and where to draw the line. By planning in advance and negotiating skillfully, you can also open the door to future work opportunities.

# 9

# Beyond a Handshake

SINCE FIRST speaking with the client, you've learned everything you could about the project and determined an appropriate fee. You've come up with a good negotiating strategy and worked out a deal that is acceptable to both you and your client. At last you are ready to start the job.

Not so fast! You have one more task to do before plunging into the assignment. You need to summarize your agreement in writing.

You may protest, "That's not necessary. I trust this client. We shook hands on the deal. Besides, time's wasting, and I'm anxious to get started so I can meet the deadline."

I've sung the same tune, but I've never regretted the time taken to finalize a deal in writing. It takes not more than an hour or so for the uncomplicated type of work I do, and even less if the client prepares the paperwork. And occasionally a contract has proven to be more valuable than I could have imagined.

A contract once rescued me when the Internal Revenue Service notified me that I owed taxes on royalties. The IRS indicated the name of the company that had filed the royalty statement and the dollar amount. I had indeed done a job for that company in the year in question, and I had been paid the very amount the IRS claimed was royalties. But the income was not royalties; it was a fee for writing an article. Fortunately, the contract clearly stated that I was to receive the sum in question as a "fee for service" (meaning that the writer is paid upon submission of the work, the rights to which belong to the publisher; therefore, no royalties are earned). I sent a copy of this contract to the IRS, along with a letter suggesting that the company had filled out the 1099 report incorrectly, entering my fee on the royalties line. I never again heard from the tax collector on this matter.

## Must I?

Having said that it is important to put the deal in writing, I must confess that I don't always heed my own advice. Most self-employed people do in fact omit this step from time to time, especially when working with a client they know well. And ninety-nine times out of a hundred, nothing horrendous happens. So why bother?

If you ask corporate lawyers why they go to the trouble of preparing a contract, they'll say that they want a legal document should they ever need to haul a consultant into court. Their contracts clearly reflect this attitude: page after page swearing the consultant to secrecy regarding the internal workings of the company; a menacing clause claiming that the consultant will incur any and all costs of legal action; and similar intimidating documents. And the contract is likely to be biased in other ways in favor of the company. As a writer, I have often been presented with contracts that assign the copyright to the publisher, meaning that the company can use my work over and over without paying me a red cent beyond the original fee.

I will sign a long and threatening contract drawn up by corporate attorneys, provided it doesn't endanger my business or force me to agree to something I find inappropriate. However, I think such documents are missing the point. Surely the main purpose of a contract or a letter of agreement is to make certain that both client and consultant know the terms of the deal. By *terms* I don't mean just the fee. In fact, money is usually only a small segment of a contract or letter of agreement. Mainly, a well-conceived document focuses on what the consultant will do and also on what the client will do to expedite the job. Although your responsibilities and those of your client may not be preceded by dollar signs, they directly affect the appropriateness of your fee. If you have to do more than you anticipated when you made your bid, the payment may not be adequate, especially if you're working for a flat project fee.

As soon as the contract or letter of agreement is drafted, both the consultant and the client should review it to be certain it accurately spells out the work that must be done, the work timetable, and the payment schedule. If critical information is incorrect or absent, the document should be amended before work is begun. Should a disagreement arise later, the terms in the contract will prevail.

Given that the main purpose of a contract or letter of agreement is to solidify the deal beyond a handshake, consider the circumstances in which it is mandatory to have such a document:

- *When you have had many discussions about a project, especially if the terms have changed repeatedly.* You want to be sure you and your client concur on what you ultimately agreed on.

- *When you are working with a new client or one who does not know your business well.* Putting your agreement in writing will help ensure that nobody is making assumptions the other party is not aware of.

- *When you and your client have agreed to share costs or responsibilities.* A written agreement ensures that both parties know who is doing what.

- *When the work must be done according to a strict timetable.* Including the schedule in the contract holds everyone's feet to the fire.

- *When third parties are involved.* If you are engaged in a subcontracting arrangement, be sure everyone understands where each party's responsibility begins and ends. Clearly stipulate who will be paying and supervising the subcontracted help.

- *When your payment includes some form of nonmonetary compensation.* Because clients are not used to payment except in the form of money, they may forget the non-monetary award. If you care about this part of your compensation enough to trade it for cash, you want to be sure you get it.

- *When you have reason to believe, or simply suspect, that the client may not uphold the bargain.* Trust your instincts. If you think the client may welsh on the deal, you want to have a document that will stand up in a court of law should you ever have to go that route to collect your payment.

Because several of these criteria were present when Kim, an outplacement consultant, was dealing with a company planning major layoffs, she knew she needed a contract. The company had never worked with an outplacement counselor before, and they had several discussions with Kim about the services she could provide. When Kim saw the contract the client had prepared, she was grateful that the terms were clarified before she began to work for the organization. The contract stipulated dates on which she was supposed to come to the company's office to provide individual counseling—days that had never been pinpointed during their talks. She had previous commitments on some of these days, for which she presented alternatives when she returned the contract. Also, Kim had offered to refer the client, if desired, to other professionals who could provide vocational testing. The client had erroneously assumed that the testing itself was included in her fee. Kim therefore reworded the contract to reflect that she would provide only the names of vocational testers, making it clear that the company had to engage and pay for these services separately.

## Letters of Agreement

You don't need to depend on a client's legal department or hire a lawyer yourself to write a contract every time you are about to start a new job. Usually you can create an appropriate document yourself, in the form of a letter of agreement.

As a piece of business correspondence, a letter of agreement can be couched in ordinary terms rather than legal language. Don't wait for the client to show the initiative. After you have shaken on the deal, take a few moments to summarize it in writing.

An uncomplicated agreement can be documented with an informal letter of just a paragraph or so, written on letterhead (yours or the client's). Here is a sample of a letter (without the customary addresses and signature line) written by a consulting accountant:

> I enjoyed talking with you today, and I look forward to going over your books. As we agreed, I will report to your office at 9 A.M. on Tuesday, January 12. The audit should take two or three days. My per diem rate is $1,200 ($600 for a day of four hours or less), payable immediately upon completion of the audit. Please contact me at once if you need to make any changes to this arrangement.

A more complicated agreement requires a more detailed letter. In addition, the client's acceptance of the terms should be actively solicited; the passive "call me if there's a problem" approach in the informal letter is not enough. Ascertain the client's acceptance of the terms by asking for a signed copy of the letter. Because the signature is important, avoid the temptation to use e-mail. If time is of the essence, fax the letter back and forth to your client.

The letter should cover all of the following points as specifically as possible:

- The nature of the project
- What you will do
- What the client will do, including what the client will provide you to work with
- The timetable for the work

- The fee

- The payment schedule

- Who will cover which expenses

- Any specific issues you have debated and agreed upon

In addition, allow yourself an out in case the client screws up or the project expands. State that your commitment to the schedule hinges on the client's getting material to you on time. Note that your fee applies to the project as described in the letter; if the parameters of the job change, so may your fee. When predictable, describe the change in payment. For example, Dale, a computer instructor, included the following language in a letter of agreement: "The fee of $2,000 for three hours of training covers up to five people. A supplemental fee of $500 per person will be charged for each additional enrollee."

At the end of the letter, include space for both your own and your client's signatures. Make two copies and sign both before sending them to the client. Either in the letter of agreement itself or in an accompanying cover note, ask the client to sign both copies and return one to you.

Although this type of letter is more detailed than a single-paragraph informal letter of agreement, the tone can still be friendly and the language that of everyday speech. It nevertheless is as binding an agreement as a formal contract written in legalese.

To make the important points stand out, I like to use an outline format or bulleted lists rather than dense paragraphs of text (a sample appears in Figure 7). Try to limit the letter to one or two pages, but go longer if you must to cover all salient matters.

## Contracts

Depending on the nature of your work, you may prefer to use formal contracts rather than letters of agreement. If you need to clearly delineate your own or your client's rights and obligations, a binding legal contract is the way to go. The legal advisor for your business can tell you when a contract is necessary or preferable.

You or your lawyer may be able to draw up a standard contract that you can use with all clients. An excellent starting point

## Figure 7
## Letter of Agreement for Editing a Manuscript

EditPerfect
2345 Main St.
New York, NY 10010
(212) 542-3456

September 15, 1999

Dear Joe:

As we discussed, I will edit your 200-page manuscript on fertilizers. My work will be on paper (not computer disk).

I will do the following:
1. Do a major reorganization of the manuscript.
2. Indicate areas where you need to add more information.
3. Refine the grammar, correct spellings, etc.—a process known as copyediting.

You will do the following:
1. Give me two copies of the manuscript for initial edit by October 1.
2. Give me one copy of the revised manuscript to copyedit in January 2000.
3. Enter changes into the computer at both stages.
4. Pay me as indicated below.

The edit will proceed in two phases:
1. Phase 1: Major reorganization and suggestions for additions
    —to be completed within six weeks of receipt of the manuscript (or by November 15 if the manuscript is received by October 1).
2. Phase 2: Copyedit of the revised manuscript
    —to be done within three weeks of receipt of the revised manuscript (assuming it comes in January and you have paid me for Phase 1).

The total project fee is $3,000, payable in two parts:
    $2,000 for Phase 1
    $1,000 for Phase 2
Payment is due within 30 days of completion of my work at each phase.

You will pay or reimburse me for any expenses related to this project, including but not limited to messenger service, long-distance phone calls, and photocopying.

Our signatures below indicate agreement with these terms.

_____          _____
Joe Bloe (Client)        date          Moe Row (Consultant)     date

for freelancers who want to create their own contracts is *Consultant & Independent Contractor Agreements,* by attorney Stephen Fishman (see Appendix). This book and its accompanying disk contain sample contracts that consultants can adapt. Whether you use this publication for your template, create your own standard contract, or have an attorney draft a basic form, you will need to modify the contract with each use, clearly stating the specifics of the job.

The contract should include the same points covered in a letter of agreement as described earlier: what each of you will do, when the work will be done, who is responsible for expenses, how much you will earn, and when payment is due. The contract should also have lines for both you and your client to pen your signatures. In addition, a contract may include legal provisions not usually found in a letter of agreement. The following issues are typical:

- The consultant will not divulge the client's trade secrets.

- The consultant is an independent contractor, that is, responsible for all taxes on income from the work.

- The consultant (or the client, depending on the arrangement) owns specified rights to the work, such as a patent or copyright.

- Either party may terminate the contract under specified conditions. Be sure this clause also stipulates the payment that is due if the work is terminated prematurely.

- The client (or the consultant) is responsible for legal fees in the event of litigation.

## Not a Threat...Unless

Some entrepreneurs maintain that they do not like contracts, arguing that they set up an adversarial relationship between client and consultant before they have even begun to work together. I disagree; the document simply solidifies the deal. But if you are of the mind that contracts are threatening, opt instead for a letter of agreement. A letter can be friendly and nonmenacing in tone.

Some clients shun contracts because they don't want to take the time to write them or to hassle with their legal department to produce an acceptable document. If your client gives you this argument, write an "as we discussed" letter of agreement yourself. It doesn't take long, rarely more than a couple of hours and sometimes only a few minutes to jot down a paragraph.

At the opposite extreme are clients who produce long, complicated contracts filled with stipulations that appear irrelevant. Review any contract provided by a client very carefully. If it contains clauses that you find objectionable, discuss them with the client, modify them as appropriate, or cross them out. You both should initial any changes penned on a contract.

The clause that seems the most outrageous is one prohibiting a consultant from working for any possible competitor of the client. Accepting this restriction could easily put you out of business! Instead, change the wording, indicating that you will not divulge any proprietary information about your client. This means you can work for "the enemy" as long as you keep your mouth shut and don't leak trade secrets.

One final word of warning. A client who won't write a contract or letter of agreement probably either is too busy or does not know how to prepare the document. This problem can be easily resolved by writing the agreement yourself. On the other hand, if the client won't *sign* a contract or letter of agreement, be wary. I can think of only one reason not to sign such an agreement: to avoid a paper trail showing a commitment. The reluctant signer may expect you to do the work but not intend to pay you. If you don't have a signed agreement, you may have a hard time collecting your fee, even if you resort to legal action. Think carefully before digging into a job for a client who won't initial a prenuptial agreement. Is it worth the risk?

# 10

## Don't Cry Over Spilt Milk

"**I**T MIGHT have been!" are the saddest words, or so John Greenleaf Whittier wrote. Carrying this dolorous phrase a bit further, a disappointed self-employed professional might lament, "It might have been my job if only I'd priced it lower!"

How often have I heard consultants bemoan a lost job, crying, "I shouldn't have asked so much!" My response is always the same: "Wasn't your price fair? Would you really have been content with less?"

If you arrived at your price by following the processes discussed in this book, you shouldn't mourn a job that slips away. The steps outlined here ensure that your price will be reasonable for the work involved. To accept less would be to shortchange yourself. Besides, price rarely is the actual reason a job doesn't come through. Many other factors can come into play.

### The Real Reasons for Not Getting the Work

A client usually will not volunteer why you or another consultant was awarded the job. If you ask, though, you may learn why you

## Can you charge a client who calls for advice?

Suppose that Client A admires your insight and calls you occasionally between projects to ask your opinion on a thorny issue. Client B often calls long after you have turned in a project, ostensibly following up on the job but actually fishing for ideas on a new venture. Client C, who is considering you for an assignment, asks how you would handle the job. In essence, all of these clients are using your services gratis.

Usually, you cannot charge for these requests for help. Chalk the hours up to good will, or consider them nonbillable time prospecting for new business. But don't let any one client develop a habit of repeatedly using your expertise without compensation.

In a few circumstances, you can bill for brain picking. If you happen to be working for the client and are

beat the competition or why somebody else got the assignment. The reason seldom has anything to do with price. It may not even bear any semblance to a business decision.

Over the years, I have heard many reasons why this or that freelancer did or didn't land a particular contract:

- The client decided to go with a freelancer whose work was known rather than offer the job to a stranger.

- The consultant and the client were not computer compatible; another freelancer who used the same software and platform (Mac or PC) ended up with the work.

- The client decided to do the job in-house rather than engage the services of a consultant.

billing by the hour, add the time to the invoice that you have not yet written. Also, if you are asked for more than telephone input—that is, if the client wants you to put your thoughts in writing or drop by to chat—politely say, "I'd be glad to do that, but I'll have to bill you for it." Some clients will be happy to pay for your ideas; others will be turned off by your response but in any case impressed by your insistence on the value of your professional services.

You might indeed want to turn off someone who constantly takes advantage of your good will. You can't bill for 10 minutes here and 20 minutes there, but you can't necessarily afford to give away your services either. The best tactic with callers who won't leave you alone is to say, "I'd be happy to talk with you, but I'm very busy now. Maybe we could discuss this in a few days." Then don't bother to return the call. In all probability, the pest will forget whatever prompted the first call.

- The client reconsidered the scope of the job and the type of person needed to do it.

- The project was postponed or canceled.

- The consultant who got the job was geographically preferable in the client's mind. It might have been simply that the consultant's office was on the route of the client's daily commute, making it easy to drop off and pick up work.

- The freelancer who was hired had a personal link, however irrelevant, with the client: They went to the same college, their kids played on the same soccer team, and so on.

- The client's personal biases influenced the hiring decision. I once heard of someone who would consider only a male freelance writer for a story on circumcision. He argued that a woman "wouldn't understand."

- Someone was already lined up for the work from the outset. The client went through the motions of searching for the best person only for political reasons.

- The client had never intended to hire a consultant but was just fishing for new ideas and information.

None of these reasons for winning or losing an assignment has anything to do with the fee the consultant asked. In fact, money rarely is the make-or-break point in hiring decisions, whether for full-time work or for consulting positions.

## It's No Big Loss

If you don't land a job, don't jump to blame it on your price. And even if you do lose a job because of your fee, you shouldn't fret over it. On the contrary, rest assured that the fee you asked for was the right fee for the job if you followed the approach of this book. It was based on the going rate: what others in your field earn for similar work and what other clients are willing to pay. Assuming that your estimate of the time needed for the job was accurate, your price ensured that you would not work for a long period without appropriate compensation. Before you presented your fee, you determined the bottom line and you know that you ought not go any lower. As a professional, you should not accept less than professional rates.

Suppose, however, that the price did play a part in the client's hiring decision. Maybe the consultant who was awarded the job did indeed ask for less. Could that freelancer be someone whose work is not up to your standards and therefore commands less? Or perhaps the competitor does excellent work but, unlike you, underestimated the scope of the project. That person may eventually come to regret accepting a job for too low a rate. Meanwhile, you are available for more lucrative work.

## More on the Second Rule of Pricing

Chapter 8 introduced the second rule of pricing for independent contractors: Determine your bottom line before quoting a fee, and never agree to work for less than the lowest acceptable rate. That rule can be expanded to address the psychology of a failed bid:

> *Addendum to Rule No. 2. Do not regret losing a job*
> *that pays less than you know it—and you—are worth.*

Sure, it's hard to lose a job you had counted on. Give yourself a little time to mourn—about twenty minutes. But don't keep beating yourself up.

Remember, you probably didn't lose the job because your fee was too high. So many other explanations, many of them totally capricious, are likely. If you keep making the mistake of blaming your bidding technique, you'll start to feel that you are not worth as much as you truly are. You may eventually come to doubt your own abilities. And you may even start to lower your rates—even though you should always aim to raise your fees.

## A Change in Attitude

Years ago I knew a freelance proofreader whom I always thought of as Gloomy Gus. Although he'd been proofreading for more than twenty years, his fees were at the very bottom of the payscale. He had little confidence in himself or his ability to bring in new clients. Instead he stayed with his old clients and raised his fees only minimally, at five-year intervals. When I first met him, the going rate for general proofreading was $12 to $15 an hour, but Gus was charging a mere $10. New clients were scared away when they learned his rate, assuming that because he charged so little, he couldn't be much of a proofreader.

One day Gus called me for advice. "I've been approached by a new client to proofread a medical book. Since medicine is your field, I thought I'd bounce a fee off you. Normally I charge $10 an hour. But because I've never done anything in medicine, I thought I'd charge $9. What do you think?"

"Are you crazy?" I exploded. "You've been proofreading *how* long and you want to *lower* your fee? So what if you've never worked in medicine! Proofreading is proofreading, no matter the field. And $10 an hour is too low. You ought to be charging at least $12, and even as much as $15 given all your years in the business."

Gus whined, "But I'm afraid I'll lose the job if I ask too much."

"You could lose it if you ask too little," I told him. "You're charging beginners' rates, and the client is probably looking for a pro."

Gus thought about that before calling back the client. He asked for $12 an hour—and got the job.

The result was much more significant than that job: Gus started to develop a new attitude. He finally realized that he'd been giving away his services, so he began to raise his rates. Much to his surprise, his offers were not rejected any more frequently than they had been when he charged less. Gus became more confident, and more bold. When a client turned him down, he swallowed hard and asked why. Never did a client say it was because he was charging too much. So Gus kept raising his rates.

After proofreading the one book, Gus realized that he wasn't thrilled with medical texts. But he did enjoy the handsome check he received for that job and the bigger checks that accompanied subsequent work for other clients at higher fees. He therefore decided to specialize in an area that pays top dollar. Today, Gus is proofreading for the financial services industry, making about $40 an hour. However, he charges the general publishing clients for whom he still occasionally works only $20, because $40 is beyond the acceptable range for that market segment. And now, when Gus loses a job he doesn't sweat it. He knows what his services should fetch and willingly shuns clients who do not recognize that he is a professional worth every penny he asks.

# 11

# How Well Did You Do?

Let's now make a giant leap in time to the point when you have finished the project. Depending on the nature of the job, many weeks or months may have elapsed since you first discussed it with the client. By now you're tired of looking at it and thinking about it. You're anxious to clean off the remnants from your workspace and file it away forever. But wait! You have one more thing to do before packing it away. You should analyze your pricing strategy.

By reviewing your pricing decisions with 20/20 hindsight, you'll be learning in the best way possible: from your own experience. The smartest ways to hone your pricing skills are to discover your weaknesses in fee setting and to replicate your successes.

Even if you did not charge by the hour, use your earnings per hour to evaluate your take. This will give you a common basis for comparing the current experience with other work situations. By now you know the formula: Convert your income into an hourly rate equivalent by subtracting your expenses from your gross fee and then dividing the net income by the number of hours you worked. All the information you need for this calculation should be in the records you've kept for the project.

Once you have calculated your hourly rate equivalent, compare it with several other hourly rates:

- Your standard hourly fee, if you have one

- What you had hoped to earn per hour on this job

- What you would have earned if you had charged on a different basis

## Revisiting the Pricing Rules

Basically, what you are doing in this final analysis is going back to square one. When you were in the process of deciding what to charge, you gathered as much information as you could about the job and considered several pricing options, such as an hourly rate, a per diem, a percentage, or a project fee. Once you had determined the appropriate rate for the circumstances, you considered strategies for negotiating the highest possible fee in case the client balked at your first offer. After you completed these steps, referred to earlier as Rule No. 1 and Rule No. 2, you presented your bid. What you now are looking at is how well you applied these two rules of pricing.

In this scrutiny of your pricing prowess you'll be crunching numbers in a variety of what-if analyses. What if I had chosen a different method of pricing? What if I had not overlooked a particular aspect of the job when determining my fee? What if I had been a tougher negotiator? In the process, you'll be asking yourself other specific questions. These will vary according to the circumstances, but the typical questions run along these lines:

- Would I have done better charging by the hour instead of assessing a flat fee?

- Would a per diem rate have made more sense for this particular job?

- Was the fee the client dictated fair for the amount of work involved?

- Did I get all the information I needed to price the job appropriately? Did I use it wisely?

- Did I omit important tasks when estimating how long it would take to do the work? How did any such omissions affect my income?

- Did I overlook certain expenses that ate into my earnings?

- Did I give in too easily when the client rejected my initial offer?

- Was my bottom line—the lowest price I felt appropriate for this job—too low?

## Analysis in Action

End-of-job income analysis is a creative process that can go in many directions. Because it does not fit neatly into a tabular format, we'll have to resort to number-riddled text as we work through an example. This case has deliberately been made a bit complicated to demonstrate the extent to which you can assess your pricing skills. In all probability you won't need to go into such depth in analyzing all your projects.

The freelancer in this case, Bob, was until a few years ago a copy editor for the publishing industry. Then he bought a computer, convinced of its potential to raise his income to a new level. After taking courses in desktop publishing he was able to leverage his knowledge of traditional publishing to become a versatile consultant who offers editing as well as design and production services. Now clients flock to him because of the excellence of his one-stop operation.

Bob just finished a project for a nonprofit association that hired him to copyedit and produce a heavily illustrated book for its upcoming thirtieth anniversary. The client told him that the book was to consist of sixty pages, with two pages highlighting each year in the history of the organization. Despite the client's assurances that the material was in a digital format compatible with his computer platform, before naming his price Bob asked for a disk to verify the compatibility and assess the amount of work involved. The material did indeed appear to be in good shape editorially, and Bob's software could handle the client's disk without a hitch. After browsing through it for a while and reviewing logs for similar copyediting and desktop publishing jobs, Bob figured that it would take him about two hours to copyedit and produce each two-page spread.

Bob hoped to average $65 an hour for the entire job, his usual desktop publishing rate for this type of assignment, but much more than his usual copyediting rate. He initially toyed with the notion of charging a page rate of $65, which would translate into $65 an hour if his time estimate was on target. But the client had indicated a preference for a project rate, so Bob set about determining a project fee.

Bob began calculating a project rate at $4,000 ($65 per hour or $65 per page multiplied by 60 pages, rounded up). Then he added a $400 cushion for client meetings and other working hours not easily allocable on a page-by-page basis. To cover expenses he allowed a generous $400. This brought his final bid to $4,800. He decided to start the negotiation process at $5,000. Because he felt that his expense allowance was more than ample, he estimated that he could come down, in stages, to a bottom line of $4,500 if the client objected too strenuously.

When Bob presented his project fee of $5,000, the client was taken aback. Bob immediately offered to shave $200 off the top, but the client wouldn't bite. To his explanation that photostats and camera work could mount up and his fee had to be high enough to cover all such costs, the client responded that consultants' fees and production expenses are two separate budget lines in the association's books. If Bob would be willing to lower his fee and submit his bills for reimbursement, they might be able to work out a deal. At this point Bob could feel the job slipping away. He sensed that if he didn't lower his fee dramatically, the client would find someone else to do the job for less. So instead of stopping at his original bottom line of $4,500, he came down to $4,300, with the understanding that the company would absorb the costs of photostats, printing, and the like. The client accepted this final offer, and they signed a letter of agreement to seal the deal.

The job went fairly smoothly, except for two glitches. The client wanted a larger say in the design of the book than Bob had anticipated, which required him to visit the association's offices on several occasions and rethink the layout after each meeting. In addition, the book grew to seventy-two pages with the covers, front matter, a time line, and an appendix describing the organization's programs and services. The copyediting went quickly, however, and once he had an approved design, Bob sailed through the desktop output part of the job. He hoped that picking up the pace would compensate for the glitches.

The day he turned in the final product, Bob tallied his hours on the job: seventy, or ten hours more than he had estimated. With trepidation, he calculated his hourly rate equivalent:

$$\$4,300 \div 70 = \$61.43$$

This figure was less than the $65 an hour Bob had hoped to earn.

Bob then considered his earnings if he had billed on an hourly basis. Charging $65 an hour, he would have made $4,550 ($65 x 70 hours), or $250 more than his total project fee. However, an astute client (and this one was quite sharp, especially regarding money) would have insisted on a lower fee for copyediting. If Bob had had to charge just $30 for the twenty-five hours he spent editing and $65 for the forty-five hours of desktop publishing, he would have earned only $3,675. In the final analysis, by assessing a flat project rate rather than an hourly fee by task, Bob came out $625 ahead, for a gain of 15 percent. He was therefore pleased with his decision to price by the project.

But then Bob came upon the notes he had made when first determining his price. He had begun by hoping to earn a page rate of $65. His project rate was based on this goal and on the understanding that the book would be sixty pages long. Of course, it had grown to seventy-two pages. Bob could have kicked himself for not realizing that the book was certain to be bigger than the client's assumption of two pages for each year in the life of the company. Bob then calculated his earnings per page: an average of $59.72 for each of the seventy-two pages, or some $5 less than his target. Had he asked for a page fee rather than a project rate, he could have charged $4,680 ($65 × 72 pages), or $380 more than the project rate he negotiated.

# Can you change your fee after you've begun a job if it turns out not to be what you were led to believe?

You can try to change your fee, but don't expect a favorable response. The rate that your client agreed to is probably as much as you'll get. That's why it's so important to learn all you can about a job before you talk price.

If there are too many unknowns when you are determining your fee, build safeguards or "wiggle room" into your offer that will allow you to amend the price. These fee-altering circumstances must be written into the contract that you and your client sign. Without something in writing, you haven't a leg to stand on.

The safeguards vary according to the job. Examples include the following:

- Your fee will be such-and-such. If the job description changes, you will renegotiate your fee.

- Your fee covers a specified time (either the number of hours or the weeks on a calendar).

The hourly rate equivalent with the page-rate method of pricing would have been $66.86 ($4,680 ÷ 70 hours), above his goal of $65 an hour and $5.43 an hour more than he earned with his project fee.

Finally, Bob recalled the negotiating process. He had come way down from his original bid of $5,000 and had settled for a figure below his bottom line of $4,500. Had he stuck with that bottom line, he would have averaged $64.29 for each of the seventy hours and $62.50 for each of the seventy-two pages. The problem was that Bob's bottom line had no padding, and he cheated himself by stepping below it.

If the job extends beyond this, commitments to other clients may make it difficult for you to finish the work. However, you will accommodate the client for an additional fee.

- You will work a specific number of hours for a stated flat fee. If you need to put in additional hours, they will be billed separately at a certain specified rate.

- Your hourly rate will be so-and-so, provided the job consists of certain specific tasks. If additional tasks that command higher rates are added to the job description, you will charge more for that work.

Don't wait until the job is done to spring a request for more money on the client. Present your case as soon as you realize that additional compensation is appropriate, and give the client time to respond. Negotiate the extra payment with the same finesse you showed when negotiating the original deal.

## Be Your Own Best Teacher

At this point you may find your eyes glazing over at these paragraphs filled with numbers, and you may be thinking, "What's the big deal? You're quibbling about a few dollars—not enough to sweat over." Yes, Bob's business isn't going to fold because he earned a few dollars less than he had hoped. Over time, though, a few dollars here and a few there will mount up. If Bob were to repeat his pricing flaws over and over during the course of a year, his annual income could be thousands of dollars short of his target.

But don't dwell too much on the figures derived in the end-of-job analysis. They simply quantify the quality of a consultant's pricing approach. The real purpose of this analysis is not to juggle numbers but to uncover one's own pricing strengths and weaknesses.

Bob's analysis revealed several important points about the way he had analyzed the information related to this job, determined his price, and arrived at a final fee:

• He did not rely enough on his knowledge of the business. He was smart to check the disk before setting his fee. But he should have realized that the book would consist of more than the two pages per year of history that the client described.

• Bob based his project fee in part on a page rate—using a page count that was too low. He would have been better off assessing a page rate, because his charge would have mounted as the page count went up. Alternatively, he could have written into the contract a clause allowing him to increase his project fee, such as: "This fee is based on the understanding that the book will be sixty pages. If it is longer, a supplemental fee of $65 per page will be added for each page in excess of sixty pages."

• Bob's time estimate was fairly accurate. Although he anticipated that the job would take sixty hours, he based this assumption on his ability to produce a page an hour. As we have seen, the job actually took seventy hours, but the book totaled seventy-two pages, not the sixty he had assumed. So it actually did take him, on average, about an hour to complete each page.

• Bob wisely added cushions to his rough project fee estimate (which he had based on the anticipated number of hours and the presumed number of pages). These cushions were not padding; they allowed for expenses and for time not allocable by page. With these adjustments, Bob's initial bid was $1,000 more than his rough estimate. Had he stuck with his original negotiating strategy, he would have been fine.

• Bob failed to hold to his bottom line. Before talking with the client, he had decided to go no lower than $4,500. Then he panicked and lowered his price to $4,300. This may not seem like a big drop, but it was lower than he knew he should go. If he had held firm to his bottom line of $4,500, his hourly rate equivalent would have come close to the $65 an hour he desired.

• A $65 fee was Bob's usual hourly rate for desktop publishing services. However, this job involved copyediting as well as desktop publishing. By pricing the job based on the more lucrative work, Bob did exceptionally well on a task for which he usually earned a much lower rate.

This analysis reveals mistakes, as well as sensible approaches, in pricing the job. By performing this type of analysis at the end of each project, you can have immediate access to information that will be useful in pricing future jobs more successfully.

## Lessons from My Own Analyses

I first learned the value of end-of-project analyses while working on the staff of a magazine. Each month, the entire staff would gather for a postmortem when an issue came off the presses. We dissected the issue from cover to cover, discussing what was great and what had gone wrong with each article. At the end of the session, we returned to our desks, buoyed by the review. We could prove that last month's stellar performance was not a fluke; we were on a roll! Or, if we had flubbed an issue, we could rectify the shortcomings we had identified with the next installment.

When I began my own business, it thus seemed natural to do a postmortem at the end of a job. A freelance editor or writer doesn't always see the finished product, however, and on the occasions when sample copies do arrive, months may have passed since the work was completed. A postmortem is best performed before mental rigor mortis sets in. So instead of dissecting my prose, I analyzed my work habits and how they were affecting my income.

Such end-of-job analyses have helped me work smarter and have brought me more money in subsequent jobs. The basic self-improvement exercise usually takes less than an hour and is so valuable that I wouldn't think of skipping it. This is why I'm always amazed at how few hands go up when I ask in my pricing workshops, "Who among you reexamines your pricing decision at the end of a job?"

In addition to the types of discoveries that the desktop publisher Bob made during his end-of-job analysis, my self-scrutiny has taught me certain critical facts about the way I work and the way I price:

- I sometimes omit important tasks when estimating how long a job will take. I first committed this error early in my freelance career, in the days when a typewriter was my only office equipment. My time estimate for calculating a project fee allowed for drafting an article, editing it, and revising it again. Because I compose at the keyboard, the initial typing was subsumed in the drafting estimate. Twice I edited the paper and retyped it, but I failed to account for both stints at the typewriter in my time estimate. As a result, I didn't make the high hourly rate equivalent I desired and my fee was barely adequate. I never again forgot to account for retyping time, even when I switched to a computer, which made revisions much quicker.

- I have forgotten to project expenses, which ate up my gross income until it was only a small net. Having made this mistake a few times, I now am careful to add potential expenses to a flat fee or to arrange in advance for reimbursement.

- Sometimes I fail to gather all the information I need about a job. More often, I learn important facts but neglect to account for them during the planning process. Once, for example, a client with a Macintosh computer was unable to read my IBM-compatible disk, despite his assertions that his computer could handle anything. We spent hours sending material back and forth by messenger, fax, and e-mail—after I had submitted my invoice, thinking the job was done. Yet I forgot this experience a year later when working with another client who used a Mac. Again I wasted several hours trying to persuade our computers to talk to each

other—unbillable hours I had not included when estimating the time needed for the job.

- I've found that page rates or fees per article that some
  clients set, which may at first appear stingy, were actually profitable when translated into an hourly rate
  equivalent. But other client-dictated fees that initially
  appeared generous turned out to be inadequate because
  the job required so many more hours than projected.

- I once learned in an end-of-job analysis that unit pricing
  would have made me richer than the project rate I'd
  assessed for writing a series of abstracts. Thus, the next
  time I had a similar job, I opted for unit pricing. I drafted
  sixty abstracts and was expecting to submit a bill after
  revising them for sixty times the unit price. But the client
  decided that the publication was too long and cut it to
  only forty-eight abstracts. Although my total fee was
  satisfactory my hourly rate equivalent was not, because I
  could not bill for the twelve dead abstracts. Now, if I use
  unit pricing for a job like this, the contract clearly stipulates that the fee is for each unit *drafted*, regardless of the
  number used, or that each draft will be billed separately
  at a portion (such as one-half) of the unit fee. With the
  latter approach, I could have charged sixty times half the
  unit price for the first draft plus forty-eight times half the
  unit price for the second draft.

- When doing similar work repeatedly, a consultant should
  be able to build up speed and work more efficiently. This
  was the case with a newsletter I wrote for four years. The
  first few issues had a steep learning curve because I had to
  become familiar with the audience and the resources
  available. By about the sixth issue, however, I was logging
  fewer hours. Because the project fee remained unchanged,
  my hourly rate equivalent grew with experience.

- To my surprise, increased efficiency was not the story
  for a series of articles I wrote for a different client, who

paid by the page. I logged more time on the fifth and sixth articles than I did on the third and fourth, so my hourly rate equivalent dipped. When I studied my project logs for the later articles, I uncovered a distinct change in a long-established pattern. Usually, I can edit a draft in half the time it takes to write it, although a difficult article could require as much revising as drafting time. In this case, the project logs for the low-yield articles showed that the editing was taking two or three times as long as the drafting. Because the projects were fresh in my mind, I knew why. I had begun writing before I had all the material, so I'd needed to add a lot of information and do extensive rewriting in the editing phase. Because I'd procrastinated and had put off the research, to make the deadline I'd had to start writing before completing all the background reading. I learned my lesson: literally, laziness doesn't pay.

- Sometimes during an end-of-job analysis I consider a different scenario: subcontracting a portion of the job. I calculate the savings in time and figure a fair subcontractor's fee that would still allow me to make decent money. This exercise helps me understand what tasks can be given out and what to pay any help should I decide to engage the services of other freelancers.

- Publishing professionals who either bill or pay by the hour will tell you that writing commands more than editing. Analysis of my project rate jobs, however, repeatedly reveals that my hourly rate equivalent for editing can be just as high as that for writing. As a result, I feel confident in raising my editing charges to match my hourly writing fees.

This is one way to raise your rates, as Chapter 13 explains. In effect, you raise your rates without even knowing it by pricing a job using a variety of methods and opting more often for approaches that yield the highest hourly rate equivalents. If for no other reason than to identify such methods, end-of-job analysis is valuable.

Analyzing a project at its conclusion can teach you much about your pricing expertise and reveal areas that need improvement. This review doesn't take long, and the rewards can be great. In addition, analyzing pricing decisions across clients, methods of charging, and other variables helps self-employed professionals discover patterns in their price-setting and working strategies that are both beneficial and detrimental to their business's success. The next chapter explains how to do this type of across-the-board analysis.

# 12

# Was It a Good Year?

THE PREVIOUS chapter explained how to evaluate your pricing techniques at the end of a job. Over the course of a year, you will do end-of-job analyses over and over as you wind down each project. These evaluations provide information that you can use to price your next projects more profitably. You'll discover even more by looking for patterns in the entire range of your work experience over an extended period of time. This across-the-board analysis can be performed on any occasion. The end of the year is a logical point, because you probably will be tallying your earnings then anyhow in preparation for paying your fourth-quarter income-tax estimate.

Once you have calculated your gross income for the year, ask yourself these key questions:

- Did you meet your annual income goal?

- How do this year's earnings compare with last year's?

- Has your total income been going up steadily over time?

- What do you want to earn next year?

The next step in year-end analysis is harder: examining how you achieved your year's income. To rework a familiar metaphor, you've seen the forest; you've even seen the trees. Now you're ready to look at the trees in groves to see how they come together to create the woods as a whole.

## How to Judge the Forest

Anyone who has gone hiking has probably noticed that a forest is made up not only of trees but of microenvironments: a dense tract of pines here, a clearing there, an elm grove in the distance, a few birches by a river below. The forest of your work is similarly composed not only of the individual trees (i.e., projects) that you analyze as you go along but also of groupings that share some common theme. The common element may be the client, the type of work, or the pricing method. To gain a picture of the forest as a whole, look at the related groupings. For example, analyze your income by:

- Individual clients, totaling your earnings on all projects undertaken for each client during the year, or for whatever period you are examining

- The type of client, such as corporations, nonprofit associations, government agencies, and individuals who engage your services

- The pricing method (e.g., hourly, project, per diem)

- The type of work, if you are a multitalented entrepreneur who offers a variety of services

- The place where you do the work, such as your own office versus a client's premises

You are by now well acquainted with the basic tool to perform this analysis: the hourly rate equivalent. By converting all your earnings to this common denominator, you will be able to compare the elm stands in your work forest with the maple, pine, and hickory groves.

The easiest way to organize this analysis, especially if you are undertaking it at year-end, is by client. If you are like most self-employed professionals, you probably close your year's books by totaling the income received from each client. You will compare your records with the 1099s that will trickle in over the next month or so to be certain that your clients have not relayed erroneous data to the Internal Revenue Service. To do your self-examination, you will need to calculate, besides your total earnings from each client, the two other components of the hourly rate equivalent: the total costs you covered without reimbursement and the number of hours you worked for each client.*

Once you have this information, calculate your hourly rate equivalent for each client. Then determine the overall hourly rate equivalent for the entire year by dividing your net income from all clients by the hours logged on every job. How do your earnings from each client compare with your overall average fee per hour?

You can also examine your income by other variables, such as the pricing method or the type of work. If you want to do additional analyses, you may need to reorganize the information or gather more data from your project logs. Suppose, for example, that I wanted to compare my average hourly fee as an editor with my hourly rate equivalent as a writer. Clients usually hire me either to write or to edit, but a few send both editing and writing projects my way. To do the analysis in question, I note which jobs from such clients were editing work and which were writing. I calculate the hourly rate equivalent for editing separately from that for writing for the few clients who think of me as an editorial jack-of-all-trades. Then I add these numbers to the earnings from other editing and writing clients to determine my overall fees by skill.

---

* I simplify data gathering by keeping a separate 5 " × 8 " card for each client. When I bill a job, I enter the relevant numbers on the client card. At the end of the year, I simply total the hours logged on each card and the income from each client. Other consultants maintain a notebook that is organized similarly, or create a computer database. Entering the numbers as you go saves time during the year-end analysis, because you don't have to wade through stacks of project folders to retrieve individual job logs.

The benefits of examining the forest of your work are numerous. Use your analyses to help you determine:

- Which clients to keep

- Which clients you should consider dropping

- What type of work is most profitable for you

- What type of work is least lucrative when examined by hourly rate equivalent

- Which pricing methods yield you the highest income

- Which pricing techniques are consistent losers

- How to raise your rates

## A Word Processor's Forest

Let's see how Jenny, a freelance word processor, analyzed a year's income. Figure 8 is the first worksheet she used for this evaluation. (All her clients reimbursed her for out-of-pocket costs, so her gross income was the same as her net income.)

This word processor earned $29,000 during the year, working only 935 hours (she tries to do her typing mainly when her children are in school). Thus, her overall hourly rate equivalent was $31. She earned slightly more than her average from her top-grossing client (Client A), who kept her on a monthly retainer of $600, and a little more than that from Client B, whom she charged an hourly fee of $35. Her take was similar for an individual (Client H), who paid her $900 on a project basis. Work for all of her other clients earned her either substantially more or considerably less than her overall hourly rate equivalent. She earned as much as $50 an hour and as little as $20 an hour.

To learn why her earnings were so variable, Jenny looked at several factors that distinguished her workload: the pricing method, the type of client, and the place where she did the typing. A pattern that she had noticed in earlier years recurred: she always topped her average hourly rate by working for corporate clients. Knowing that the market will bear more in the corporate sector, she has

## Figure 8
## A Word Processor's Year-end Evaluation of All Clients

| Client | Gross (Net) Income | Total Hours | Hourly Rate Equivalent | Pricing Method | Type of Client | Where Worked |
|--------|------|------|------|------|------|------|
| A | $7,200 | 225 | $32 | Retainer* | Corporate | Client |
| B | $6,300 | 180 | $35 | Hour | Corporate | Home |
| C | $5,000 | 200 | $25 | Hour | Nonprofit | Home |
| D | $3,000 | 75 | $40 | Per diem† | Corporate | Client |
| E | $2,200 | 100 | $22 | Project | Nonprofit | Home |
| F | $1,200 | 30 | $40 | Project | Individual | Home |
| G | $1,000 | 24 | $42 | Per diem† | Nonprofit | Client |
| H | $900 | 25 | $36 | Project | Individual | Client |
| I | $800 | 32 | $25 | Hour | Individual | Home |
| J | $600 | 12 | $50 | Project | Corporate | Home |
| K | $300 | 15 | $20 | Project | Individual | Home |
| L | $300 | 12 | $25 | Hour | Individual | Home |
| M | $200 | 5 | $40 | Hour‡ | Individual | Home |

|  | Total |  | Average§ |
|--|-------|--|----------|
|  | $29,000 | 935 | $31 |

* $600/month.
† $250/day.
‡ Weekend rush rate.
§ Average hourly rate equivalent is computed by dividing total income by total hours.

made her standard hourly fee $35 for corporate clients and $25 for nonprofit associations and individuals who engage her services. She often used other methods of pricing with the latter types of clients, hoping to earn a high hourly rate equivalent. The strategy worked wonderfully when she charged Client G a $250 per diem; this nonprofit was her second-highest-paying client when ranked by hourly rate equivalent. Project fees were profitable for two individuals who hired her (clients F and H) but yielded considerably less than her standard hourly fee for clients E and K. Finally, Jenny looked at where she did her word processing and saw that she usually earned more per hour working in her clients' offices, away from the distractions of home.

## Close-up of the Forest's Highlights

Most freelancers have some clients that represent large proportions of their workload and others that are occasional callers or one-shot deals. After looking at your experience with all of your clients, no matter how small, to discover patterns in your pricing and working strategies, focus more on the big guys. They are the ones responsible for most of your working hours and most of your income.

Ideally, the percentage of total income earned from a client will equal or exceed the percentage of all your working hours devoted to that client. In other words, you want your relative earnings from a client to at least match the amount of time you work for that client. If you spend 40 percent of your time working for a client that represents only 20 percent of your income, something is terribly wrong.

As she continued her year-end analysis, therefore, Jenny turned her attention to clients A through E. These were the clients responsible for most of her income during the year, as well as for the bulk of her working hours. She calculated the percentage of her total annual income and the percentage of all her logged time from these five clients. She reviewed her pricing experiences with each of these clients and noted where changes were in order. Her calculations and the comments she made during this analysis are shown in Figure 9.

The ratios of time to earnings were fairly good for Jenny's five most important clients. The percentage figures for income and hours were practically identical for Client A, from whom she grossed the most money. Focusing on that client, though, Jenny realized that her retainer did not produce an hourly rate equivalent as high as the hourly rate she could be charging this corporate client.

Client C was another problem, representing 21 percent of her working time but only 17 percent of her income. Previously, Jenny had had a similar experience with Client D. By changing

### Figure 9
### A Word Processor's Year-end Major Client* Evaluation

| Client | Percent of Total Income | Percent of Total Hours | Comments |
|---|---|---|---|
| A | 25 | 24 | Hourly rate equivalent ($32) less than standard corporate hourly rate ($35). Raise retainer? |
| B | 22 | 19 | Good client. No change needed. |
| C | 17 | 21 | Need to raise rate. Pad hours? Use different pay method? |
| D | 10 | 8 | Hourly rate equivalent ($40) with per diem better than last year's hourly charge ($35). |
| E | 8 | 11 | Need to set higher project rates, change pay method, or drop client. |

* Totals 82 percent of annual income.

her method of billing this client—from an hourly fee to a per diem—Jenny had tipped the balance to make working for Client D more profitable. As part of her year-end analysis, Jenny noted some strategies to make Client C a more lucrative proposition. She also considered better approaches to Client E and raised the possibility of dropping this marginal business, which represented only 8 percent of her income.

Jenny learned a lot in both her year-end review of her overall experience and the more intense scrutiny of her major clients. Knowing the following facts, Jenny can now pick her clients better and be a more shrewd biller:

- Her services were worth $31 an hour on average.

- Corporate clients were the best payers, nonprofit associations generally the worst.

- The retainer for Jenny's main client, while it slightly topped her overall hourly rate equivalent, earned her less than she could make from this client if she billed by the hour.

- A per diem of $250 resulted in a better-than-average hourly rate and enabled Jenny to earn top dollar from a major corporate employer (Client D) and a nonprofit group (Client G).

- Her project rates often were profitable, but Jenny could stand to hone her project-pricing skills.

- Working in a client's office was a better deal for Jenny than working in her own home office.

## A Quick Stroll Through My Own Year-End Analyses

I always look forward to doing year-end analyses. It's interesting to see how my clients stack up next to each other and to discover patterns I didn't know existed. Most of the time, these analyses provide excellent guidance to improve my earnings and my business in general. Yet every now and then I choose to ignore the message.

The most blatant example of going against my own better judgment was one time when I decided to part company with my highest-paying client, which I'll identify by the pseudonym Raleigh. According to the numbers, Raleigh was a winner in every way. My total income was higher from this client than from any other, the hourly rate equivalent was at the top for my editing jobs, and I made 32 percent of my year's income from Raleigh in only 24 percent of my billable hours. The analysis indicated that this client was one I should keep at all costs. But the costs were proving too great. My main contact at Raleigh drove me nuts! He couldn't keep to a schedule, and the work came to me days or even weeks after it was due. I found myself always rearranging my workload and putting off other clients because of Raleigh. My nemesis there argued with me constantly, playing childish games like "My phrasing's better than yours" and "Ha! You missed the typo." To show who was boss, he would demand, "You'll do it this way because I said so!" The aggravation was becoming unbearable, the hours I lost because of it substantial but unbillable. Consequently, although my year-end analysis said not to do it, I dropped the client. (As it turned out, I made up the lost income from other clients who were far more pleasant to work with and who paid just as well. But you never know if it will turn out that way. That's one of the risks of self-employment.)

Usually, I follow the lessons of my year-end self-examination, especially when consistent patterns emerge over several years. Discoveries in my year-end analyses have changed how I price and how I conduct my business. Consider these examples:

• *Project fees almost always turn out to be my best bet.* I saw this pattern early in my consulting career. Other freelancers told me that project rates were their worst approach. The more I applied my technique for setting project rates, the more I recognized its logic and value. I refined it, developed a course in setting project rates, and am now sharing the approach with you. Whenever it makes sense and the client is amenable, I opt for a project fee.

• *Working in-house is always a losing proposition for me, even if the rate seems adequate.* Freelance editors, especially copy editors, are often asked to work in the client's office. From time to time I used to accept such assignments on a steady basis. I have worked in-house for an hourly fee, a per diem, and a retainer, all of which seemed appropriate at the time the client engaged my services. But on every year-end analysis, the in-house work was at the bottom of the list when I ranked my clients by hourly rate equivalent. Now I refuse to take on any long-term in-house job, although I might be persuaded to work in a client's office for a day here and there.

• *I work surprisingly few hours over the course of a year.* I am always amazed when I total my billable hours. Rarely do they exceed 1,200 over the span of a year. One year, when I felt I was working nonstop, I logged something like 1,700 billable hours, which averages only 34 hours a week in a 50-week year. I know I can take on much more work than I do. I'll explain why I am so "lazy" in Chapter 14.

• *I can earn as much for editing as for writing—or more.* My year-end analysis usually includes a column for task or skill. Over the years, I have learned that I can make as much money for editing as for writing, especially when I price editing work on some basis other than an hourly rate. This discovery defies conventional wisdom, which ranks writing as a more lucrative profession than editing. Knowing that I have earned top dollar in the past for editing, I feel justified in aiming high.

• *My services are worth more than I have charged.* My year-end analyses show a wide span in hourly rate equivalents. Every year I discover that some clients are paying me three times as much as others and twice as much as my standard hourly fee. I know from this exercise that my services are worth more than I have led myself—and my clients—to believe. Encouraged by this knowledge, I have raised my rates.

That is the greatest benefit of making year-end assessments: they will help you raise your rates. The next chapter explains how to use your year-end reviews to increase your fees.

# 13

## Give Yourself a Raise

Most of us have been taught from childhood that modesty is a virtue. We learn that you can't put a price tag on people. Then, when we start our own business, we realize that we have to attach prices to ourselves; if we are too modest, the business won't be successful. This conflict between upbringing and career aspirations is why it's so hard to price our services to begin with and to increase our fees as we go along.

When it comes time to raise our rates, we self-employed entrepreneurs behave just like Dagwood Bumstead approaching Mr. Dithers. We sweat and stew and lose sleep until finally we dare to bring up the subject with the boss—ourselves.

Some consultants lessen the agony by setting up formulas for raising their rates. They match the government-declared increase in the cost of living, or hike their fees to meet their growing expenses. Other independent contractors watch industry trends and set their fees according to the prevailing earnings of their salaried counterparts. To avoid constantly approaching clients for more money, some freelancers raise their rates on a schedule, such as every other year, every third year, or once every five years. (No kidding. I know excellent freelancers who have increased their fees less than half a dozen times in the twenty years or more that they have had their own businesses. Meanwhile, more assertive competitors with half their talent are earning twice as much.)

Here is a different approach for raising your rates. With this technique, your fees will be going up all the time, but you won't have to agonize over the process. In fact, much of the time you won't be consciously raising your rates; they'll go up without your being aware of it. When you do actively change your prices, your higher fees will be based not only on your own idea of the value of your services but on your clients' estimation of your worth as well.

## Gleaning More from Your Year-End Analyses

If you're at a loss as to what your services are worth, you need look no further than your latest year-end analyses. There you'll discover what your clients feel your work merits. You will find not only the average value of your services, as reflected in the overall hourly rate equivalent from all your clients, but also the highest rates that your best clients willingly paid.

Basing your charges on other people's notion of the value of your services, as reflected in your year-end analyses, helps you leap the modesty hurdle. Clients are willing to pay what they think you are worth. Even if you aren't certain that your work is so valuable, somebody else thinks that it is.

If you can get $75 an hour from one client, why should you be content with $35 from another? Not every client will be as generous as your top payer, who may have resources so vast that what you consider a windfall barely makes a dent in the client's budget. But you should aim at least for a rate in the middle range of your real-life experience (otherwise known as your overall or average hourly rate equivalent).

By focusing on your overall average rates as well as your top earnings, you play a mind game with yourself. The game will give you the courage to set your rates higher. This is a game you are bound to win.

Consider Marion's story. She had been charging $50 an hour for her consulting services. She made more than that, however, by charging a flat fee, working for a per diem rate, or assessing a percentage of the client's increased business that was directly attributable to her work. As a result, her overall average hourly rate equivalent was $59. Realizing this, she started to think of herself not as a $50-an-hour entrepreneur but as a $60-an-hour pro. When new clients inquired about her hourly fee, she told them $60. She conquered her anxiety about quoting the higher fee by reminding herself that her best client the previous year had paid her the equivalent of $85 an hour, and her effective hourly rates from other top payers were $75 and $70. Marion also raised her per diem rate from $400 to $500 to reflect her new understanding of the value of her time. When calculating project rates, she multiplied her anticipated hours by $60 instead of $50. As a result, by her next year-end review, her overall hourly rate equivalent had risen to $66.

## Making the Right Moves

Raising your rates is not just a head game. You have to take concrete steps to make the numbers go up. Follow these tips:

- If your hourly fee is less than your overall hourly rate equivalent from the past year or two, raise your standard hourly rate to that level. Don't lower it, however, if your hourly rate equivalent for some reason is less than your standard fee. Always aim higher.

- When appropriate, use separate hourly fees for categories of higher- and lower-paying clients. Legitimate categories are types of work and industry segments, such as corporate and nonprofit sectors. Stingy and generous are not appropriate groupings for fee structures.

- Choose pricing methods that pay the best when translated into an hourly rate equivalent, even if doing so means introducing old clients to a new price basis. Your

year-end analyses will indicate your most lucrative
pricing methods.

- Use a higher hourly fee to calculate an appropriate per
  diem or project fee. When using a multiple-rate system
  to calculate a project fee, multiply the hours you expect
  to log by your old hourly rate and by a new, higher fee.
  The products of these two calculations will be, respec-
  tively, the minimum you should ask and a higher target
  that's right for a consultant who can command more
  per hour than your previous self.

- When starting business with new clients, quote higher
  fees than you've been charging old standbys.

- Consider dropping low-paying clients—whether individuals or types of employers. The negative effect of a
  poor payer extends beyond the work you do for that
  client. It also lowers the average when you calculate the
  overall hourly rate equivalent in your year-end analysis.
  Future fees based on that average will not be as high as
  they would have been if you hadn't included that fee.
  And from a psychological point of view, a more modest
  overall hourly rate equivalent may make you think you're
  not worth as much as you really are.

These approaches helped Jenny, the freelance word processor
introduced in the previous chapter, to raise her rates. She already knew
that corporations were willing to pay more for her services than other
clients, so she charged them $10 an hour more. The year-end analysis
in Figure 8 (page 125) revealed that individual clients for whom she
worked often valued her services more than she had realized. The
average take from the six individuals who hired her that year was $31,
identical to her overall average. She therefore decided to expand her
hourly fee structure from two categories to three: $35 for corporate
clients, $30 for individuals, and $25 for nonprofits. One nonprofit in
the year reviewed felt that she was worth a lot more; this client paid
her a per diem fee of $250. To try to gain the most from other
nonprofits, Jenny decided to try per diem billing more often. She also
planned to use a target of $30 per hour when calculating project fees
for both nonprofit organizations and individual clients.

## Charting the Course

If you play the pricing game well, with passing years your gross income as well as your annual hourly rate equivalent should display an upward trend. You may have a year when you slip back or simply hold the course. But by and large, your revenue and rates should be going up—just like the salaries or wages of staff employees whose boss determines their pay.

An interesting exercise is to chart your freelance salary and wage history. It may be difficult to reconstruct this experience if you have not kept appropriate records in the past, but you can start to create your chart with the current year. Record your annual income and overall hourly rate equivalent, along with the changes you made to boost your income. After a few years, note the patterns. Are your average rates going up? What changes in your business practices were effective in raising your rates? What steps can you take in the future to increase your income?

Ricardo, a self-employed financial planner, has kept such a record for the five years he has been in business. Figure 10 (page 136) shows how his analysis of his business shortcomings and his plans to improve the picture have shaped his earnings. With planning, his gross income went up $13,000 between his first and fourth years. In general, his average hourly rate equivalent has been rising, although the progression has not been linear. Each hour of labor now earns him 29 percent more than when he hung up his shingle five years ago, inflation aside. Ricardo isn't earning more by accident. He increases his hourly charge whenever two successive years of experience convince him that his rising hourly rate equivalent is not a fluke. He experiments with various methods of pricing and makes changes when they are not proving lucrative. And hoping to earn more, he keeps altering his client and product mix. Ricardo has worked to make his business a success and is reaping the rewards of a higher income.

## More for Less

Charging more gives you confidence in your business capabilities and helps you weather any storm. One of the scariest threats to the self-employed is the forces over which you have no control, such as a general slowdown in the economy. Entrepreneurs who

# Figure 10
## Salary and Wage History of a Self-Employed Financial Planner

Year 1. Gross income: $65,000. Overall hourly rate equivalent: $55.

*Changes from past:*
Not enough. Based consulting fee
on most recent staff salary.

*Plans for future:*
Raise hourly fee to $60.
Don't give away so much. Limit
free introductory session
to one hour.

Year 2. Gross income: $73,000. Overall hourly rate equivalent: $65.

*Changes from past:*
Raised hourly fee to $60.
Limited free introductory session
to one hour.
Did initial review with new
computer software.

*Plans for future:*
Attract more high-net-worth
clients; charge them percentage fee.

Year 3. Gross income: $69,000. Overall hourly rate equivalent: $66.

*Changes from past:*
Charged flat fee for computer-
based review; not high enough.
Tried percentage fee; not lucrative
with mid-level clients.

*Plans for future:*
Raise flat fee for computer-
based review.
Raise hourly fee to $65.
Don't use percentage fee unless
client's net worth > $500,000.

Year 4. Gross income: $78,000. Overall hourly rate equivalent: $74.

*Changes from past:*
Stopped working with clients
worth < $100,000.
Attracted more clients worth
> $500,000.
Used percentage fee only for clients
worth > $500,000.
Raised fee for computer-based review.
Raised hourly rate to $65.

*Plans for future:*
Explore related services to offer.
Get new software.
Hold fees steady for now.

Year 5. Gross income: $71,000. Overall hourly rate equivalent: $71.

*Changes from past:*
Most new clients worth $100,000–
$500,000.
Offered insurance products; haven't
recouped start-up costs.

*Plans for future:*
Raise hourly fee to $70.
Find more clients worth
> $500,000.
Take out ads in professional
journals?
If can't bring in enough insurance
business, get out within two years.

have been steadily raising their rates may find, amazingly, that they may actually make more per hour when the economy sours, business slows, and their gross income slips. Even in a bad year, they realize, their services are highly valued.

Peter, a sales consultant, earned $80,000 one year by working regular forty-hour weeks, taking off only two weeks for vacation. That year, he logged 2,000 hours, for an hourly rate equivalent of $40. The next year the economy slumped and his gross income dropped to $66,000. He worked only 1,100 hours that year, but, to his surprise, this yielded him a much higher hourly rate equivalent of $60. Despite anxiety about his reduced gross income, Peter relished the extra time he had for his favorite pastime, sailing.

Then the recession reversed and Peter's business picked up. His attitude, meanwhile, underwent a major about-face. He now realized that his services were really worth closer to $60 an hour, not the meager $40 he had earned in a "good" year of steady work. Accordingly, he raised his rates, quoting an hourly fee of $50 to old clients who called on him again after an absence of a year or longer, and $60 to newcomers. He also relied on other methods of pricing, hoping to earn even more. In the third year of this story, he grossed $81,000 while working only 1,500 hours—because he decided to keep his summers free for sailing.

Other freelancers have discovered the same benefit of raising their fees. In fact, this is one of the greatest advantages of entrepreneurship. As your rates go up, you may be able to bring in the same annual income as in the past, or more, even though you are working fewer billable hours. The extra time is yours to do with as you wish. You may decide to devote the time to business development, or you might pursue personal ventures.

In both your business and personal lives, you set the priorities. Whether or not money is high on your own list, you should be able to attain your desired income while freeing yourself for the other things that really matter, provided you have set your fees high enough.

# 14

## It's up to You

**I**'VE NOW shared all I know about pricing—at least at the moment; every day I learn something new. Even as I was writing this book, I gained new insights into the question that all consultants repeatedly face: What should I charge? One such realization is that fee setting is both a science and an art. As in other scientific endeavors, rules must be followed and particular steps taken to assure a successful outcome. The art in pricing is reflected in the consultant's creativity when taking those steps. Every successful pricing decision is a scientific and an artistic masterpiece in its own right.

### Pricing as a Science

A scientist does not launch into experimentation at random. The process is directed toward a goal: to prove a hypothesis. Adhering to a protocol or series of prescribed steps, the scientist collects data, analyzes the findings, and concludes that the facts either support the hypothesis or do not.

When you enter the laboratory of price setting, you too will have a goal: to make the most money possible under the circumstances.

To achieve this goal, you will also follow the series of steps we've analyzed earlier:

- You learn as much as you can about the job.
- You attempt to discover the going rate for this type of work.
- You consider different methods of pricing and select the most logical choices.
- In all probability, you consult past project logs to determine how long the job might take.
- Based on all the information you obtained in the previous steps, you calculate a fee.
- You determine your opening bid, the lowest acceptable fee, and your negotiating points, in case the client does not respond favorably to your first offer.
- After you and the client have come to an agreement, you summarize it in writing.
- As you do the work, you keep a project log, noting how long you spend on each task and what out-of-pocket costs you incur.
- After completing the job, you analyze your fee-setting strategy, looking for what you did right and where you went wrong.

A few of these steps are so critical that I have incorporated them into what I consider the only hard-and-fast rules of pricing. Applying these two rules consistently will ensure the success of your fee-setting experiments:

> *Rule No. 1—Never quote a price on the spot. First get as much information as you can about a job. Then take time to assess the project thoroughly and calculate the best rate.*

> *Rule No. 2—Before quoting a fee, determine the lowest acceptable rate—and the concessions to stipulate if you have to go that low. Never agree to work for less than you know a job is worth and your services merit. Do not regret losing a job that pays less than you know it—and you—are worth.*

## Pricing as an Art

No matter how closely you follow these steps and how strictly you apply the two rules, it's the art of pricing that turns a good business into an outstanding one. Unlike a scientific discipline, art is too creative a process to summarize in a list of bulleted points. Art is an attitude, an approach, a novel way of looking at the world. Because pricing is an art as well as a science, no job has only one correct fee. Your creative approach may be vastly different from that of your competitor, and a good price for you may be a losing deal for the guy across town.

Rely on your creative instincts at every step of the pricing process. Don't be afraid to try something different. A pricing method that you have never used before, or one that has not so far proven stellar in your hands, may yet be the perfect solution for the unique circumstances of a new job. If it isn't, you'll have other opportunities during the year to make up for any losses.

Let your imagination run free as you manipulate the tools of the pricing trade. Try modifying my template for project logs to create records that will give you the most mileage. And be especially creative in the negotiating process. Only you know what you want from a job, in terms of both money and nonfinancial rewards. You can achieve whatever goals you set for your business by following the logical steps in the science of fee setting and adding your own artistic flourishes.

## Going for the Goals

I can't overemphasize the importance of having goals. Without a goal in mind, you can run tests, but you won't prove a thing; you can dab paint on a canvas, but you won't create a picture. Having goals keeps a business from just plodding along from year to year. Goals give you a target to direct your business's growth.

Every business owner should have financial goals. How much do you need to meet your monthly expenses? How much do you want to earn this year? In addition, most entrepreneurs have equally important goals that are not preceded by dollar signs. Some of your objectives will remain the same as long as you are in business. Other goals will change over time as you achieve your aims and consider new directions.

In my first year as a freelancer, my goal was to bring in as many clients as possible so that I wouldn't have to worry about running out of work. By the second year, I had more clients than I could handle comfortably and was hooked on self-employment. Then my goal changed: I wanted to earn more than I could make at a staff job so that I would never again have to consider working for someone else. I attained that goal too. In my third year in business, because I was making good money and had plenty of work, I decided to sift out the deadwood: the low-paying, irritating clients who were dragging me down. Again I accomplished my goal, and my income increased as a result.

Meanwhile, I was becoming heavily involved in an organization of professional peers. Given the hours I was devoting to this volunteer work, could I keep my business running smoothly and profitably? When the annual rate survey of my peer group was published, I was pleased to see that my income was once again in the top quartile.

Family obligations intermittently drew my attention away from business for several years. I hoped to keep my income at its previous level despite these distractions, and I achieved this goal. I was particularly proud of my high gross during a year in which I practically became a commuter between my New York office and my family homestead in Chicago.

After this personally hectic period, my approach to my business underwent a major upheaval. I was tired of working constantly! I never had time for things that were in no way connected to my business. By zeroing in on the best-paying clients and raising my rates significantly, I was able to give myself days—even weeks—off to pursue my pleasures. Although I worked fewer hours, I made more money than I had when I was running myself ragged. I found I could be a successful freelancer and a well-rounded person at the same time. That is still my primary goal.

## True Confessions

Because I have decided to limit my billable hours, I am a far cry from the wealthiest freelancer in my professional niche. My gross income is only half that of my most successful colleagues who work 50-hour weeks (but twice that of stereotypical struggling freelancers I know). My fees are fair, though, and my earnings on each project are exactly what I want them to be. I simply don't take on enough work to bring my annual income to the top of the heap, because I have chosen not to.

But I am making good money—by practicing price setting as a science and an art. More important (or so I think at this point), I am living the kind of life I want. I have given myself time to follow my dreams: writing novels, one of which I hope will be published someday; enjoying the cultural treasures of New York, the most exciting city in this country; and writing this book.

I often remind myself what Frank Sinatra used to sing about my chosen city: "If I can make it there, I'll make it anywhere. It's up to you, New York, New York."

Whether you're in New York or Peoria, your business can be as successful as you want. Simply put, it's up to you.

# *Appendix*

# *Resources*

This appendix lists publications, Web sites, and organizations you might want to explore. It is by no means a comprehensive resource list. These listings are merely starting points to direct you to resources for help in managing your business. As an independent businessperson, you presumably know how to use such leads to begin searching for information and contacts.

## Books

I spent many hours in bookstores, the library, and on the Web trying to identify useful books on pricing for consultants. Much to my surprise, I came up empty. Filling this void was a major motivation for writing this book.

The larger bookstores in my area have eight or more shelves devoted to small businesses. Most of the books in this section are geared to people who are launching a home-based career. Nearly all these volumes contain a chapter on fee setting, but it typically runs only ten to twenty pages. Although you might find some of these books interesting if you are starting your own consultancy, you won't learn much from them about pricing. And established freelancers will find little useful information in the start-up books.

The books described below are the best at the time of this writing. They are directed to both established and budding entrepreneurs. These books offer solid advice on business management in general and on issues related to pricing. (The page counts and price information in the bibliographic sections are approximate.)

Biech, Elaine. *The Business of Consulting: The Basics and Beyond.* San Francisco: Jossey-Bass/Pfeiffer, 1999. 245 pages, including disk. $40.

Without question, this is the best book for consultants who are serious about their business and are true entrepreneurs. It is informative, practical, and easy to read. The author is a professional trainer, and her book reflects this perspective. Money matters are discussed in two chapters, about one-fifth of the text. All the forms in the book can be retrieved from the accompanying disk and customized for personal use.

Fishman, Stephen. *Consultant & Independent Contractor Agreements.* Berkeley: Nolo Press, 1998. 280 pages, including disk. $25.

This book, by an attorney, is directed as much to clients as to consultants. The publication and accompanying disk provide sample contract forms and clear explanations of the various clauses. In addition to general consultant and independent contractor agreements, contracts for specific types of entrepreneurs—including accountants, software consultants, and creative types—are included. In all cases, one contract is provided for clients, another for consultants. The contracts can be photocopied or taken off the disk, which is compatible with Windows 95, Windows 3.1, DOS, and Mac systems.

Ruhl, Janet. *Answers for Computer Contractors.* Leverett, Mass.: Technion Books, 1999. 210 pages. $30.

Written specifically for computer professionals, this book contains good general information about consulting and contracting. The chapter on fees includes data from a recent survey of computer specialists and confirms a huge spread in rates.

Shenson, Howard L. *The Contract and Fee-Setting Guide for Consultants and Professionals.* New York: Wiley, 1990. 260 pages. $28.

Before the more recent books described above, this was the one must-read text recommended by consultants, who had found in it a good reference for self-employed professionals. The book contains solid advice to enhance the professionalism of an individual's business. The emphasis is on proposals and contracts, with less than fifty pages devoted to fees.

Tepper, Ron. *The Consultant's Proposal, Fee, and Contract Problem-Solver.* New York: Wiley, 1993. 245 pages. $25.

This book, slightly better than most other general volumes that didn't make the cut for this listing, is not nearly as good as the Shenson volume and is typical of other books that purport to discuss fees. Pricing is confined to a mere twenty pages. About twenty sample contracts are presented.

## Magazines

A number of magazines are geared toward entrepreneurs and small-business owners. Most have articles on business management, and they may publish fee-setting stories from time to time. The following list of periodicals that the self-employed may enjoy gives the name of the publication, its tagline, the 1999 newsstand price, and the Web site, if available.

*Home Office Computing.* $3.99. www.smalloffice.com

*Inc.* The magazine for growing companies. $3.50. www.inc.com

*Opportunity World.* The ultimate survival magazine for start-up business entrepreneurs. $2.99.

*Small Business Opportunities.* Money-making ideas for entrepreneurs. $3.25.

*Success.* The leading magazine for entrepreneurs. $3.95.
www.successmagazine.com

## The Internet

The computer is a great resource for self-employed professionals.
Instead of making scores of phone calls, mailing handfuls of letters, or spending hours in the library, you may be able to find
information you need in a few minutes on the Web.

I am hesitant to provide Web sites or even directions to start
you on a computer search, because the dynamic realm of
cyberspace will certainly change by the time you read this book.
Yet we cannot ignore this 21st-century mode of operation. So
here are some preliminaries.

Start with your Internet provider. America Online, for example, organizes information by "channels," one of which is called
"workplace." Click on it and you'll find leads to specific types of
work, including home-based businesses and start-ups. Through
"consulting" message boards you can chat online with other AOL
subscribers who are consultants. CompuServe provides similar
connections through its "forums," including ones called "business," "work-at-home," and "business dynamics." Many of the
messages exchanged there concern pricing and related issues. After exhausting your Internet provider's exclusive services, go to a
search engine like Yahoo or Netscape.

A few general suggestions:

- Useful keywords for Internet searches include "consulting," "freelance," and the name of your specialty. You
  can also try Boolean searches like "consultant AND
  pricing."

- If you know of an association of professional peers (see
  the next page), you may be able to find it on the Web
  by entering its acronym followed by .org or .com.

- Follow links to related Web sites to expand your search.

## Professional Organizations

As a self-employed person, you have probably become used to working alone, but that doesn't mean you have to be completely on your own. Professional organizations provide networks for information sharing and problem solving. Your colleagues in these groups may be the best sources of advice on pricing.

The following list may help you locate a professional organization of interest. If none of these fifty-nine groups seems relevant to the type of work you do, try identifying an appropriate organization through the *Encyclopedia of Associations*, which can be found in most larger libraries. Or enter your specialty into your computer's search engine and see what turns up.

American Association of Attorney-Certified Public Accountants (AAA-CPA)
24196 Alicia Pkwy., Suite K
Mission Viejo, CA 92691
Phone: (949) 768-0336
Web site: www.attorney-cpa.com

American Association of Insurance Management Consultants (AAIMCO)
c/o Anna Shuherk
Famet, Inc.
17 Aldrich Rd.
Columbus, OH 43214-2623
Phone: (614) 261-0552

American Association of Language Specialists (TAALS)
1000 Connecticut Ave. NW, Suite 9
Washington, DC 20036
Phone: (301) 986-1542
Web site: www.TAALS.net

American Business Women's Association (ABWA)
9100 Ward Pkwy.
PO Box 8728
Kansas City, MO 64114-0728
Phone: (816) 361-6621
Fax: (816) 361-4991
E-mail: info@abwahq.org
Web site: www.abwahq.org

American Center for Design
325 W. Huron St., Suite 711
Chicago, IL 60610
Phone: (800) 257-8657; (312) 787-2018
Fax: (312) 649-9518
E-mail: members@ac4d.org
Web site: www.ac4d.org

American Design Drafting Association (ADDA)
PO Box 11937
Columbia, SC 29211
Phone: (803) 771-0008
Fax: (803) 771-4272
E-mail: national@adda.org
Web site: www.adda.org

American Home Business Association (AHBA)
4505 S. Wasatch Blvd., No. 140
Salt Lake City, UT 84124
Phone: (801) 273-2350
Fax: (801) 273-5422

American Institute of Certified Public Accountants (AICPA)
1211 Avenue of the Americas
New York, NY 10036-8775
Phone: (800) 862-4272; (212) 596-6200
Fax: (212) 596-6213
Web site: www.aicpa.org

American Institute of Graphic Arts (AIGA)
164 Fifth Ave.
New York, NY 10010
Phone: (800) 548-1634; (212) 807-1990
Fax: (212) 807-1799
Web site: www.aiga.org

American Society for Training and Development (ASTD)
Box 1443
1640 King St.
Alexandria, VA 22313
Phone: (703) 683-8100
Fax: (703) 683-8103
Web site: www.astd.org

American Society of Indexers (ASI)
PO Box 39366
Phoenix, AZ 85069-9366
Phone: (602) 979-5514
Fax: (602) 530-4088
E-mail: info@ASIndexing.org
Web site: www.ASIndexing.org

American Society of Interior Designers (ASID)
608 Massachusetts Ave. NE
Washington, DC 20002
Phone: (202) 546-3480
Fax: (202) 546-3240
Web site: www.asid.org

American Society of Journalists and Authors (ASJA)
1501 Broadway, Suite 302
New York, NY 10036
Phone: (212) 997-0947
Fax: (212) 768-7414
Web site: www.asja.org

American Society of Media Photographers (ASMP)
14 Washington Rd., Suite 502
Princeton Junction, NJ 08550-1033
Phone: (609) 799-8300
Fax: (609) 799-2233
Web site: www.asmp.org

American Society of Tax Professionals (ASTP)
PO Box 1213
Lynnwood, WA 98046-1213
Phone: (877) 674-1996
Fax: (425) 672-0461

American Society of Women Accountants (ASWA)
60 Revere Dr., Suite 500
Northbrook, IL 60062
Phone: (800) 326-2163; (847) 205-1029
Fax: (847) 480-9282
E-mail: aswa@aswa.org
Web site: www.aswa.org

American Translators Association (ATA)
1800 Diagonal Rd., Suite 220
Alexandria, VA 22314
Phone: (703) 683-6100
Fax: (703) 683-6122
E-mail: ata@atanet.org
Web site: www.atanet.org

American Woman's Society of Certified Public Accountants
(AWSCPA)
401 N. Michigan Ave.
Chicago, IL 60611
Phone: (800) 297-2721; (312) 644-6610
Fax: (312) 321-6869
E-mail: awscpa_hq@sba.com
Web site: www.awscpa.org

Associated Writing Programs (AWP)
George Mason University
Tallwood House, Mail Stop 1E3
Fairfax, VA 22030
Phone: (703) 993-4301
Fax: (703) 993-4302
E-mail: awp@gmu.edu
Web site: www.gmu.edu/departments/awp


Association of Bridal Consultants (ABC)
200 Chestnutland Rd.
New Milford, CT 06776-2521
Phone: (800) 355-0464
Fax: (860) 354-1404
E-mail: BridalAssn@aol.com
Web site: weddingchannel.com


Association of Image Consultants International (AICI)
1000 Connecticut Ave. NW, Suite 9
Washington, DC 20036-5032
Phone: (800) 383-8831; (301) 371-9021
Fax: (301) 371-8847
E-mail: aici@worldnet.att.net
Web site: www.aici.org


Association of Part-Time Professionals (APTP)
7700 Leesburg Pike, Suite 216
Falls Church, VA 22043-2615
Phone: (703) 734-7975
Fax: (703) 734-7405
E-mail: info@aptp.org
Web site: www.aptp.org

Association of Professional Communication Consultants
(APCC)
3924 S. Troost
Tulsa, OK 74105-3329
Phone: (918) 743-4793
Web site: www.apcc-online.org

Copywriter's Council of America (CCA)
Communications Building 102
7 Putter Lane, Box 102
Middle Island, NY 11953-0102
Phone: (516) 924-8555
Fax: (516) 924-3890. Call first
E-mail: linickgrp@att.net

Editorial Freelancers Association (EFA)
71 W. 23rd St., Suite 1910
New York, NY 10010
Phone: (212) 929-5400
Fax: (212) 929-5439
E-mail: info@the-efa.org
Web site: www.the-efa.org

Graphic Artists Guild (GAG)
90 John St., Room 403
New York, NY 10038
Phone: (212) 791-3400
Fax: (212) 791-0333
Web site: www.gag.org

Graphic Communications Association (GCA)
100 Dangerfield Rd.
Alexandria, VA 22314-2888
Phone: (703) 519-8160
Fax: (703) 548-2867
Web site: www.gca.org

Guild of Natural Science Illustrators, Inc. (GNSI)
PO Box 652, Ben Franklin Station
Washington, DC 20044
Phone: (301) 309-1514
Fax: (301) 309-1514
E-mail: gnsihome@HIS.com

Home-Based Working Moms (HBWM)
PO Box 500164
Austin, TX 78750
Phone: (512) 266-0900
E-mail: hbwm@hbwm.com
Web site: www.hbwm.com

Independent Computer Consultants Association (ICCA)
11131 S. Towne Square, Suite F
St. Louis, MO 63123
Phone: (800) 774-4222; (314) 892-1675
Fax: (314) 487-1345
Web site: www.icca.org

Independent Educational Consultants Association (IECA)
3251 Old Lee Highway, Suite 510
Fairfax, VA 22030-4106
Phone: (800) 808-IECA; (703) 591-4850
Fax: (703) 591-4860
E-mail: IECAassoc@aol.com
Web site: www.educationconsulting.org

Institute of Certified Business Counselors (ICBC)
PO Box 70326
Eugene, OR 97401
Phone: (541) 345-8064
Fax: (541) 349-0753
E-mail: cbc@continent.org

Institute of Certified Financial Planners
3801 E. Florida Ave., Suite 708
Denver, CO 80210-2544
Phone: (303) 759-4900
Fax: (303) 759-0749

Institute of Internal Auditors (IIA)
249 Maitland Ave.
Altamonte Springs, FL 32701-4201
Phone: (407) 830-7600
Fax: (407) 831-5171
E-mail: custserv@theiia.org
Web site: www.theiia.org

Interior Design Society (IDS)
PO Box 2396
High Point, NC 27261
Phone: (800) 888-9590
Fax: (336) 883-1195
E-mail: IDS1@nr.infi.net
Web site: www.interiordesignsociety.org

International Association for Financial Planning (IAFP)
5775 Glenridge Dr. NE, Suite B-300
Atlanta, GA 30328-5364
Phone: (800) 945-IAFP; (404) 845-0011
Fax: (404) 845-3660
E-mail: info@iafp.org
Web site: www.iafp.org

International Association of Business Communicators (IABC)
1 Hallidie Plaza, Suite 600
San Francisco, CA 94102
Phone: (415) 433-3400
Fax: (415) 362-8762
E-mail: service_centre@IABC.com
Web site: www.IABC.com

International Association of Lighting Designers (IALD)
Suite 487, The Merchandise Mart
200 World Trade Center
Chicago, IL 60654
Phone: (312) 527-3677
Fax: (312) 527-3680
E-mail: IALD@IALD.org
Web site: www.IALD.org

International Interactive Communications Society (IICS)
39355 California St., Suite 307
Fremont, CA 94538
Phone: (510) 608-5930
Fax: (510) 608-5917
E-mail: worldhq@iics.org
Web site: www.iics.org

International Interior Design Association (IIDA)
341 Merchandise Mart
Chicago, IL 60654
Phone: (312) 467-1950
Fax: (312) 467-0779
E-mail: iidahq@iida.com
Web site: www.iida.com

Mothers' Home Business Network (MHBN)
PO Box 423
East Meadow, NY 11554
Phone: (516) 997-7394
Fax: (516) 997-0839
E-mail: momhomebiz@mhbn.com
Web site: www.homeworkingmom.com

National Association of Black Accountants, Inc. (NABA)
7249A Hanover Pkwy.
Greenbelt, MD 20770
Phone: (301) 474-6222
Fax: (301) 474-3114
Web site: www.nabainc.org

National Association of Computer Consultant Businesses
(NACCB)
715 N. Eugene St.
Greensboro, NC 27401
Phone: (336) 273-8878
Fax: (336) 273-2878
Web site: www.NACCB.org

National Association of Home Based Businesses (NAHBB)
PO Box 30220
Baltimore, MD 21270
Phone: (410) 363-3698
Web site: www.usahomebusiness.com

National Association of Independent Insurance Adjusters
(NAIIA)
300 W. Washington, Suite 805
Chicago, IL 60606
Phone: (312) 853-0808
Fax: (312) 853-3225
E-mail: assist@naiia.com
Web site: www.naiia.com

National Association of Independent Publishers (NAIP)
PO Box 430
Highland City, FL 33846-0430
Phone: (941) 648-4420
Fax: (941) 648-4420
E-mail: NAIP@aol.com

National Association of Personal Financial Advisors (NAPFA)
355 W. Dundee Rd., Suite 200
Buffalo Grove, IL 60089
Phone: (888) 333-6659
Fax: (847) 537-7740
Web site: www.napfa.org

National Association of Professional Organizers (NAPO)
1033 La Posada Dr., Suite 220
Austin, TX 78752-3880
Phone: (512) 206-0151
Fax: (512) 454-3036
E-mail: napo@assnmgmt.com
Web site: www.napo.net

National Association for the Self-Employed (NASE)
PO Box 612067
DFW Airport, TX 75261-2067
Phone: (800) 232-NASE
Fax: (800) 551-4446
Web site: www.nase.org

National Contract Management Association (NCMA)
1912 Woodford Rd.
Vienna, VA 22182
Phone: (800) 344-8096; (703) 448-9231
Fax: (703) 448-0939
Web site: www.ncmahq.org

National Court Reporters Association (NCRA)
8224 Old Courthouse Rd.
Vienna, VA 22182
Phone: (800) 272-6272; (703) 556-6272
Fax: (703) 556-6291
E-mail: msic@ncrahq.org
Web site: www.verbatimreporters.com

National Society of Accountants (NSA)
1010 N. Fairfax St.
Alexandria, VA 22314-1574
Phone: (800) 966-6679; (703) 549-6400
Fax: (703) 549-2984
Web site: www.nsacct.org

National Writers Union (NWU)
113 University Pl., 6th Floor
New York, NY 10003-4527
Phone: (212) 254-0279
Fax: (212) 254-0673
E-mail: nwu@nwu.org
Web site: www.nwu.org

Professional and Technical Consultants Association (PATCA)
PO Box 4143
Mountain View, CA 94040
Phone: (650) 903-8305
Fax: (650) 967-0995
E-mail: info@patca.org
Web site: www.patca.org

Professional Association of Resume Writers (PARW)
3637 4th St. N., Suite 330
St. Petersburg, FL 33704-1336
Phone: (800) 822-7279; (727) 821-2274
Fax: (727) 894-1277
E-mail: parwhq@aol.com
Web site: www.parw.com

Registry of Interpreters for the Deaf (RID)
8630 Fenton St., Suite 324
Silver Spring, MD 20910
Phone: (301) 608-0050
Fax: (301) 608-0508
E-mail: RIDmember@aol.com
Web site: www.RID.org

Society for Technical Communication (STC)
901 N. Stuart St., Suite 904
Arlington, VA 22203-1854
Phone: (703) 522-4114
Fax: (703) 522-2075
E-mail: stc@stc-va.org
Web site: www.stc-va.org

Type Directors Club (TDC)
60 E. 42$^{nd}$ St., Suite 721
New York, NY 10165
Phone: (212) 983-6042
Fax: (212) 983-6043
Web site: www.TDC.org

Women in Production (WIP)
347 Fifth Ave., Suite 1406
New York, NY 10016-5016
Phone: (212) 481-7793
Fax: (212) 481-7969
Web site: www.wip.org

# Index

Alterations of fees, 112–13
American Medical Writers Association (AMWA), 32, 36
annual income goals
    recording, 135
    setting, 7–8, 56–57, 141–43
assignments, not getting, 101–6
    change in attitude and, 105–6
    price and, 104
    reasons for, 57, 101–4

Billing techniques, 48–49, 50, 84–85
budgetary restraints, 2, 11, 37, 71, 72
business expenses, 8–9
    client payment for, 12, 13, 86, 88–89, 116
    hourly rate equivalent and, 19–20
    local travel, 12–13
    ongoing, 3–4, 9
    out-of-town travel, 13
    paying from project fee, 39, 49–50, 59, 63, 64, 116
    reimbursement of, 12, 13, 116
    shipping, 3–4
    start-up, 9
    taxes, 9
bylines, negotiating for, 85

163

Year-end analysis, 121–30
    examples of, 124–30, 135–37
    information gained from, 129–30, 132–33
    raising rates after, 130, 132–33
    related client groups and, 122–24
    *See also* post-project analysis

## About the Author

Laurie Lewis has had a successful freelance medical writing and editing business since 1985. A native of Chicago, she held several staff positions in the Midwest before moving to New York City and launching her own business. She has traveled from coast to coast as a consulting instructor. She is an active member of the Editorial Freelancers Association and the American Medical Writers Association.